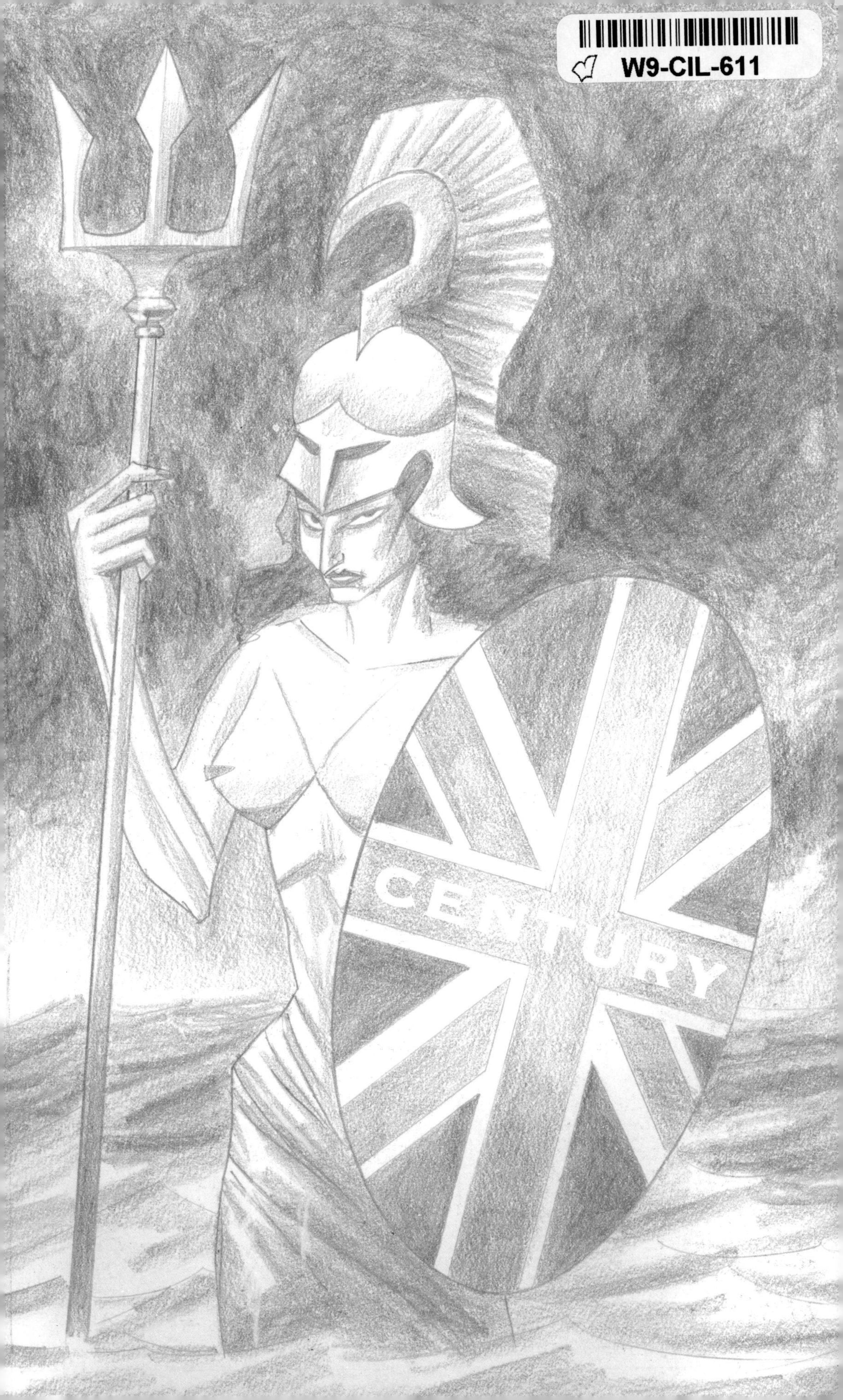
CENTURY

ROGUES IN THE GALLERY.

ALAN MOORE (Author and dandy). "They say **TODD KLEIN** designed this tat and spun his calligraphic skills on it."

KEVIN O'NEILL (Artist and probably Irish). "To be sure, **BEN DIMAGMALIW'S** colouring gilds the lily an' all."

AMERICAN PUBLISHER (Eavesdropping). "Those foolish fops will work for scraps."

CHRIS STAROS editor	TOP SHELF PRODUCTIONS Chris Staros & Brett Warnock publishers	KNOCKABOUT COMICS Tony Bennett & Josh Palmano publishers	Captain Universe is ©1954 Mick Anglo (used with permission). Special thanks to Iain Sinclair

Visit our online catalogues at www.topshelfcomix.com and www.knockabout.com

1910.

FRATERS AND SORORS...

BELOVED FRATERS AND SORORS...

WE ARE GATHERED IN THE PROFESS-HOUSE.

WE CAN BEGIN.

B-BUT OLIVER...I'M SORRY. I'M SORRY. MASTER...

MASTER, DO WE EVEN KNOW WHAT WE'RE ATTEMPTING TO CALL DOWN? WHAT IF IT'S...?

CALM YOURSELF, ILIEL.

WE WORK ONLY THE LAW. SEE FRATER CYRIL AND FRATER SIMON. DO THEY SEEM AFRAID?

OBSERVE SOROR CYBELE. DOES SHE TREMBLE?

He's right, Soror.

ALL THE MASTER'S TALKING ABOUT IS A CHILD. WHAT COULD BE MORE HARM-LESS?

QUITE. IT'S NOT THE END OF THE WORLD, SOROR ILIEL.

WELL SAID, FRATER CYRIL.

WHAT WE ARE SEEKING TO ESTABLISH HERE IS BUT THE FOUNDING STONE OF OUR INVISIBLE COLLEGE.

A *MOON*-STONE.

A MOON-*CHILD*.

AND ONCE THAT CHILD FULFILLS ITS DESTINY...

...THEN SHALL THE KINGDOMS OF THE EARTH BE PLUNGED INTO A STRANGE AND TERRIBLE NEW AEON.

1: What Keeps Mankind Alive?

ffah!

GET YOUR CLOTHES ON, LASS.

HE WANTS TO SEE YOU.

HELLO, JACK.

ਪ੍ਰਣਾਮ ਬਾਪੂ

ਤੁਹਾਡਾ ਕੀ ਹਾਲ ਐ?

MOBILIS IN MOBIL

EVENIN', MISS JANNI.

ਮੈਂ ਉੱਜ ਈ ਆਂ, ਨਾ ਅੱਗੇ ਤੋਂ ਭੈੜਾ ਨਾ ਚੰਗਾ।

ਮੈਂ ਪੁੱਛਦੀ ਆਂ ਤੁਸੀਂ ਅਪਣਾ ਇਰਾਦਾ ਬਦਲਿਆ ਐ ਜਾਂ ਨਹੀਂ?

ਭੱਲੀ ਨਾ ਹੋ

ਮੈਂ ਹਰਗਿਜ਼ ਨਹੀਂ ਬਦਲਿਆ

ਤੂੰ ਮੇਰੀ ਨਾਫ਼ਰਮਾਨੀ ਕੀਤੀ

ਤੂੰ ਆਪਣੇ ਪਿਓ ਦੀ ਨਾਫ਼ਰਮਾਨੀ ਕੀਤੀ

ਇਹ ਨਾ ਭੁੱਲ ਕਿ ਤੂੰ ਮੇਰੀ ਧੀ ਏਂ

ਨਹੀਂ

ਮੈਂ ਵੀ ਉਹ ਸਾਰੇ ਵਰ੍ਹੇ ਨਹੀਂ ਭੁੱਲੀ ਜਦੋਂ ਤੁਸੀਂ ਉੱਕਾ ਮੇਰੇ ਵੱਲ ਧਿਆਨ ਨਹੀਂ ਕੀਤਾ

ਤੁਸੀਂ ਮੇਰੇ ਵੱਲ ਧਿਆਨ ਇਸ ਲਈ ਨਹੀਂ ਕੀਤਾ ਕਿ ਤੁਹਾਨੂੰ ਪੁੱਤਰ ਚਾਹੀਦਾ ਸੀ

ਆਹੋ, ਮੈਨੂੰ ਪੁੱਤਰ ਚਾਹੀਦਾ ਸੀ ਪਰ, ਮਨੂੰ ਤੂੰ ਹੀ ਲੱਭੀ

ਤੇ ਕੀ ਤੂੰ ਮੇਰਾ ਕੰਮ ਤੇ ਮੇਰਾ ਨਾਂ ਅੱਗੇ ਟੋਰੇਂ ਗੀ?

ਵਾਹ, ਉਹ ਨਾਂ ਕੀ ਜਿਹਦੀ ਕੋਈ ਪਛਾਣ ਨਹੀਂ, ਤੇ ਉਹ ਕੰਮ ਕੀ ਜਿਹੜਾ ਜਾਅਲੀ ਐ?

ਮੈਂ ਤੇਰੇ ਵਾਂਗ ਜਨੂਨੀ ਨਹੀਂ

ਮੇਰੇ ਵੱਲੋਂ ਤੋਂ ਜਹੰਨਮ ਵਿਚ ਜਾ

HEY! CALM DOWN, CAPTAIN. YOU'LL MAKE YOURSELF BAD.

ਤੇਰੀ ਇਹ ਹਿੰਮਤ ਕਿ ਤੂੰ ਮੇਰੇ ਨਾਲ ਇੰਜ ਬੋਲੀਂ? ਤੈਨੂੰ ਛੈਂਟੀ ਲਵਾਉਣੀ ਚਾਹੀਦੀ ਐ।

:koff: :koff:

Whoa. STEADY ON NOW, YOUNG MISS JANNI.

I'D NEVER HAVE BROUGHT YOU UP HERE IF I'D KNOWN THE CAPTAIN WOULD UPSET YOU...

HE'S NOT A CAPTAIN! WHEN WAS HE IN ANY COUNTRY'S NAVY? HE'S A PRINCE WHO PLAYS WITH BOATS!

DEAR ISHMAEL, PLEASE GET OUT OF MY WAY. I'M NOT IN ANY MOOD TO TALK TO YOU TONIGHT.

WELL, FAIR ENOUGH, CHILD, BUT YOU KNOW YOUR FATHER.

IT MAY BE SOONER OR LATER, BUT HE'LL HAVE HIS WAY.

HE ALWAYS DOES.

FAR AWAY ♪ IN FOREIGN CLIMES, ♪ DEAR...

♫ I HAVE ROAMED FOR TWENTY YEARS... ♪

♪ THOUGH THEY'VE THOUGHT ME DEAD AT TIMES, DEAR... ♪♪

♪ FEW HAVE SHED ME ANY TEARS. ♪

AAA!

OH GOD...

It's...IT's ALL RIGHT. IT WAS JUST ANOTHER DREAM. I'M AWAKE NOW.

TOM?

WHAT THE DEVIL'S GOING ON?

BULLY FOR YOU.

YOU KNOW YOU'VE PROBABLY MANAGED TO WAKE UP THE THREE MUSKETEERS, DON'T YOU?

YES, PROBABLY.

GOD, A.J., I NEED A DRINK.

Uuwuhh

WELL, I SUPPOSE AT LEAST THE MOON IS ABOVE THE YARDARM, SO I'LL PROBABLY JOIN YOU.

WHAT WERE YOU DREAMING ABOUT, ANYWAY? MORE OF THIS OMINOUS STUFF THAT MINA'S SO CONCERNED OVER?

I DON'T KNOW. I ONLY REMEMBER FRAGMENTS: A SINISTER CULT, A FOREIGN GIRL SWIMMING NAKED, SOMEONE SINGING A CATCHY SONG...

PROBABLY NOTHING SIGNIFICANT.

GOOD. I'VE NEVER COTTONED TO ALL THIS MYSTICAL TOMMYROT. NO OFFENCE.

NONE TAKEN. IF MY PREMONITIONS OF A DISASTER IN LONDON HADN'T BEEN SO STRONG, I WOULDN'T BE MIXED UP WITH YOU PEOPLE EITHER.

US PEOPLE? DON'T MAKE ME LAUGH, CARNACKI. YOU'RE MORE LIKE THEM THAN I AM.

AFTER ALL, AT LEAST YOU VOLUNTEERED YOUR SERVICES. I WAS BLACK-MAILED INTO THIS WHEN THEY UNCOVERED MY BURGLARY CAREER.

HOW WOULD A DROP OF THE 1736 AMONTILLADO SUIT YOU?

JUST THE JOB.

BUT SERIOUSLY, RAFFLES, YOU'RE NOT TELLING ME YOU DON'T ENJOY ALL THIS LARK?

I MEAN, YOU SEEM TO GET ON WITH MURRAY AND QUATERMAIN JUNIOR...

THEY'RE ALL RIGHT. IT'S THAT HE-SHE.

HA HA. YES, I KNOW WHAT YOU MEAN. THAT WAS A BIT OF A SHOCK FOR ME AS WELL...

TOM...

WHAT WAS A BIT OF A SHOCK? I HOPE IT WAS WORTH WAKING EVERYBODY OVER.

Oh, CARNACKI JUST HAD ONE OF HIS NIGHTMARES. ISN'T THAT RIGHT, TOM?

Really? AND DID IT YIELD ANY CLUES TO OUR FORTHCOMING DISASTER, MR. CARNACKI?

I'M AFRAID NOT...ALTHOUGH THERE WAS SOME STUFF ABOUT A CULT OR SECT OF SOME KIND.

ACTUALLY, THINKING ABOUT IT, ONE OF THE CHAPS I DREAMED OF SEEMED TERRIBLY FAMILIAR...

WHAT A BORE. ALL THE CHAPS I DREAM OF ARE TERRIBLY *OVER*-FAMILIAR.

Oh, LANDO, DO SHUT UP.

SO, MR. CARNACKI, WHERE DID YOU RECOGNISE THE MAN IN YOUR DREAM FROM? SOME FORMER ENEMY, PERHAPS?

NO. HE WAS HOODED, BUT HE LOOKED LIKE SIMON IFF, AN OLD BOY FROM MY CHEYNE WALK CLUB.

THE ONE FULL OF DECADENTS AND OCCULTISTS?

MORNING, EVERYONE. IT IS MORNING, ISN'T IT?

WHAT'S GOING ON?

MR. CARNACKI'S HAD ANOTHER DREAM, THIS ONE ABOUT OCCULTISTS...INCLUDING ONE HE KNOWS, APPARENTLY.

TELL ME, DO YOU THINK THE SECT IN YOUR DREAM MIGHT BE PLOTTING THE DESTRUCTION IN LONDON THAT YOU FORESAW?

I SUPPOSE IT'S POSSIBLE. THEY SEEMED EXCITED ABOUT SOME PROJECT OR SCHEME...

HUH. WELL, I'LL BET LONDON'S SEEN WORSE. DID I EVER TELL YOU ABOUT HOW I HELPED FOUND LONDON? "NEW TROY" WE CALLED IT THEN...

YES, YOU'VE TOLD US. DOZENS OF TIMES, ACTUALLY.

LOOK, THE SCHEME YOU MENTION... COULD IT HAVE ANYTHING TO DO WITH THE IMMINENT CORONATION?

PERHAPS.

I REMEMBER SOMETHING ABOUT USHERING IN A DREADFUL NEW AEON...

Hmm...AND PRESUMABLY NOT THE DREADFUL NEW AEON OF GEORGE THE FIFTH?

I KNOW MILITARY INTELLIGENCE ARE WORRIED ABOUT SOME ANTI-ROYAL PLOT. ALSO, HALLEY'S COMET IS PASSING...

MINA, COME ON. YOU'RE NOT SUPERSTITIOUS, SURELY?

I DIDN'T USED TO BE, MR. RAFFLES. THAT'S WHY I HAVE TO WEAR THIS SCARF.

NO, I THINK A VISIT TO MR. CARNACKI'S CLUB MIGHT BE IN ORDER...

Hmph. I'D BETTER HAVE A SHAVE, THEN.

YOU KNOW, SHAVING EVERY DAY...I ABSOLUTELY HATE IT.

IT'S MUCH MORE TIRESOME THAN HAVING A PERIOD EVERY FEW WEEKS.

Don't you find?

♪ STILL A YOUNG MAN...

♪ ...NOT YET TWENTY...

♪ ...I'D STEP OUT AND TAKE THE AIR.

♪ AS FOR PICKINGS...

♪ ...I HAD PLENTY...

♪ ...MILLER'S COURT TO MITRE SQUARE.

...THINKING ABOUT SIGNING ON FOR CHALLENGER'S EXPEDITION DOWN PERU WAY.

HOW ABOUT YOU?

DUNNO. MIGHT TRAIN AS AN AIRSHIP PILOT. APPARENTLY, THE PAY IS...

LUCKY 'EATHER! LUCKY 'EATHER TO KEEP THE COMET AWAY!

'ERE, DID YOU SEE THE PAPER? IT SAID OLD CUFF 'AD DIED...

WHAT, THE COPPER?

YEAH. 'IM WHAT SOLVED THE MOONSTONE CAPER. HEART ATTACK, SO THE PAPER SAID...

WOTCHER, SUKI. HOW'S TRADE, DEAR?

BRISK. HARDLY STOOD UP ALL NIGHT...

...MARK MY WORDS, BUILDING BIGGER SHIPS MEANS WAR'S COMING. REMEMBER THE TITAN...

GET YER LUCKY 'EATHER!

...NEW KING? STUTTERING 'ALF-WIT MORE LIKE...

...ABOUT THAT 14TH EARL OF GURNEY, HIS SPEECH IN THE HOUSE OF LORDS? HE...

CUTTLEFISH HOTE

Staff Wanted

...ALL HALF BARMY. IT'S THEM PUBLIC SCHOOLS, LIKE GREYFRIARS...

LUCKY 'EATHER! GET YER LUCKY CORONATION 'EATHER!

...RUMOUR ABOUT THE CHATTERLYS...

...NEAR QUONG LI'S TEA SHOP IN LIME- HOUSE...

'EATHER! KEEP THE COMET AWAY WITH LUCKY 'EATHER!

ROLL UP, LADIES AND GENTLEMEN...

ROLL UP FOR THE WONDER OF THE AGE! YOU'VE 'EARD ABOUT IT! YOU'VE READ ABOUT IT!

IT TERRORIZED THE 'IGH SEAS! IT BROUGHT DOWN THE BARNES BRIDGE MARTIAN!

NOW 'ERE IT IS, LADIES AND GENTS, BEFORE YOUR VERY EYES...

I GIVE YOU THE ONE...THE ONLY... ORIGINAL...

...REPRODUC-TION OF...

...THE *NAUTILUS!*

SEE THE VESSEL THAT STRUCK FEAR IN OCEAN-GOERS EVERYWHERE!

SEE THE FEARSOME PIRATE CAPTAIN *NEMO*, BROUGHT TO LIFE AT TREMENDOUS EXPENSE!

ROLL UP!

ONE AT A TIME, PLEASE! IT'S ADULTS A BOB AND NIPPERS A TANNER.

THANK YOU VERY MUCH, SIR. ROLL UP!

THANK YOU, MADAM.

THANK YOU. THANK YOU, SIR.

ANY MORE NOW, PLEASE?

THANK YOU...

CUTTLEFISH HOTEL

Staff Wanted

Um... PLEASE EXCUSE ME?

THE SIGN OUTSIDE, IT SAYS YOU NEED WORKERS.

THAT'S RIGHT. POUND A WEEK, WITH BED AND BOARD.

WHAT'S YOUR NAME?

NO credit

Um... JANNI.

Mm-hm. WELL, JENNY, IT'S MOSTLY CLEANING WORK WHAT YOU'LL BE DOING.

WHAT'S YOUR SECOND NAME?

Temp staff Jenny

DIVER.

JENNY DIVER.

HA. WELL, WELCOME TO OUR DIVE, EH?

THE PAY'S NOT MUCH, BUT A CLEVER GIRL CAN PROSPER.

COME ON. I'LL SHOW YOU TO YOUR ROOM.

MILITARY COUP IN RURITANIA

TRINIAN

‡fffp‡

MILITARY COUP RURITANIA

TRINIAN

AH, HELLO THERE. IT'S THOMAS CARNACKI. I'M HERE FOR THE MERLIN SOCIETY MEETING.

MR. CARNACKI. OF COURSE.

AND YOUR FRIENDS?

OH, I'M SORRY. THIS IS MISS MURRAY AND MIS...MISTER ORLANDO, WHILE THIS IS MISTER QUATERMAIN, THE SON OF THE ADVENTURER.

THEY'RE MY GUESTS.

INDEED. PLEASE STEP THIS WAY.

INCIDENTALLY, MR. QUATERMAIN, I GREATLY ADMIRED YOUR FATHER. A TRAGIC LOSS.

YES. YES, IT WAS. THANK YOU.

NOT AT ALL, SIR.

YOUR COAT, MADAM?

Hmph. RUM-LOOKING CROWD, I MUST SAY.

ALLAN, DON'T BE SO PROVINCIAL.

SO, MR. CARNACKI, ARE THESE ALL OCCULTISTS?

YES, OR INVESTIGATORS OF THE UNEARTHLY. THAT'S DYSON AND PHILLIPS, AND THERE'S DEAR OLD JOHNNY SILENCE...

THE FELLOW IN THE TURBAN TALKING TO DR. TAVERNER, THAT'S PRINCE ZALESKI.

I CAN'T SEE OLD IFFY ANY-WHERE...

NEVER MIND. HOPEFULLY, A.J. IS GATHERING INTELLI-GENCE AT THIS MOMENT.

Hmm. FIRST TIME FOR EVERYTHING, I SUPPOSE.

LOOK, MINA, SINCE I KNOW IFFY, WHY DON'T ALLAN AND I LOOK FOR HIM?

YOU AND ORLANDO COULD MINGLE...

...AND PRY. GOOD IDEA.

YOU KNOW, I THINK A FORMER DOCTOR OF MINE USED TO COME HERE...

OH, LOOK! THERE'S SOMEONE *I* KNOW.

THIS IS GETTING INTERESTING.

IFF, Simon Alexander

EXCUSE ME, MR. ZANONI, ISN'T IT?

MY, um, MOTHER WAS IN FORTUNIO'S ENTOURAGE TO SEE YOUR "RITE OF SMARRA."

FORTUNIO, EH? A TRUE GENTLEMAN.

FORTUNIO HAD MET THEM ALL: THE SICILIAN, THE COUNT VON OST. ALL THE GREATS.

Mm. FASCINATING.

ACTUALLY, WE WERE LOOKING FOR A SIMON IFF...

Huh. YOU'RE NOT FRIENDS OF HIS, I HOPE?

IFF'S A SCOUNDREL. HE SIDED AGAINST ME IN MY MAGICAL WAR.

HE SIDED WITH *HADDO.*

OLIVER HADDO, THE DIABOLIST? DIDN'T HE DIE IN STAFFORDSHIRE A COUPLE OF YEARS AGO?

LET'S HOPE SO.

REPORTEDLY, HADDO WAS ATTEMPTING TO MAKE HOMUNCULI.

HOMUNCULI? WHY?

ISN'T IT OBVIOUS? HE NEEDS A MOONCHILD TO END THE WORLD.

MINA?

I'M AFRAID WE'VE DRAWN A BLANK.

SHALL WE BE GOING?

NICELY TIMED, TOM. A.J. SHOULD BE FINISHED BY NOW.

Mm. AND NOBODY HAS SEEN IFFY IN WEEKS.

LOTS OF GLOOMY TALK, THOUGH.

GLOOMY? IN WHAT WAY?

IN AN OCCULT WAY. IMMINENT DOOMSDAY FORECASTS AND THE LIKE, CONNECTED WITH THE CORONATION...

I SAY! FANCY MEETING YOU HERE.

FANCY. DID YOU FIND IFF'S FILE?

PIECE OF CAKE. I'VE GOT IT HERE.

HOW ABOUT YOU LOT? DID YOU FIND OUT ANYTHING?

NOTHING VERY CHEERFUL, I'M AFRAID.

OMINOUS THINGS ARE HAPPENING, AT LEAST ACCORDING TO PSYCHIC RUMOUR.

HAPPENING AS WE SPEAK.

Ishmael?

Oh, GOD. IS HE *BAD*, JACK?

I KNEW IT'D FINISH HIM, HER VANISHING LIKE THAT...

YOU'D BEST COME AND SEE FOR YOURSELF.

MOBILIS IN MOBILI

Oh, no. OH, CAPTAIN, *LOOK* AT YOU...

W-WE CAN'T FIND HER, SIR. WE'VE BEEN SEARCHING ALL OVER, THESE LAST WEEKS.

TH-THEY SAID THERE WAS A STEAMER PASSING AROUND THEN, BOUND FOR LONDON, BUT WE COULDN'T TELL IF...

ਇਸਮਾਈਲ

1865

ਮੇਰੀ ਕਿਸ਼ਤੀ ਨੂੰ ਕਾਲਾ ਪੇਂਟ ਕਰ ਦੇ

ਤੇ ਮੇਰੀ ਖੋਪੜੀ ਨੂੰ ਇਹਦੇ ਅੱਗੇ ਕਿੱਲ ਲਾ ਕੇ ਜੋੜ ਦੇ

ਤੇ ਇਹ ਮੇਰੀ ਧੀ ਨੂੰ ਦੇ ਦੇ।

♪ ALL MY OLD HAUNTS, THEY REMIND ME... ♪

♪ ...OF THE GIRLS I KNEW BACK THEN. ♪

♪ POOR AND HAPLESS... ♪

♪ ...LEFT BEHIND ME... ♪

♪ ...NEVER TO BE... ♪

♪ ...MET AGAIN. ♪

♪ THERE WERE CATHYS... ...THERE WERE MARYS... ...LEFT FOR CONSTABLES TO FIND...

...WHILE I SAILED FOR BUENOS ARES...

♪ ...OUT OF SIGHT... ...AND OUT OF MIND.

TWENTY YEARS I'VE BEEN AWAY, DEAR... ♪

...WHY, IT'S HARDLY CHANGED AT ALL.

HARD-UP WOMEN GET NO SAY, DEAR... ♪

♪ ...RENTS GO UP... ...AND KNICKERS FALL.

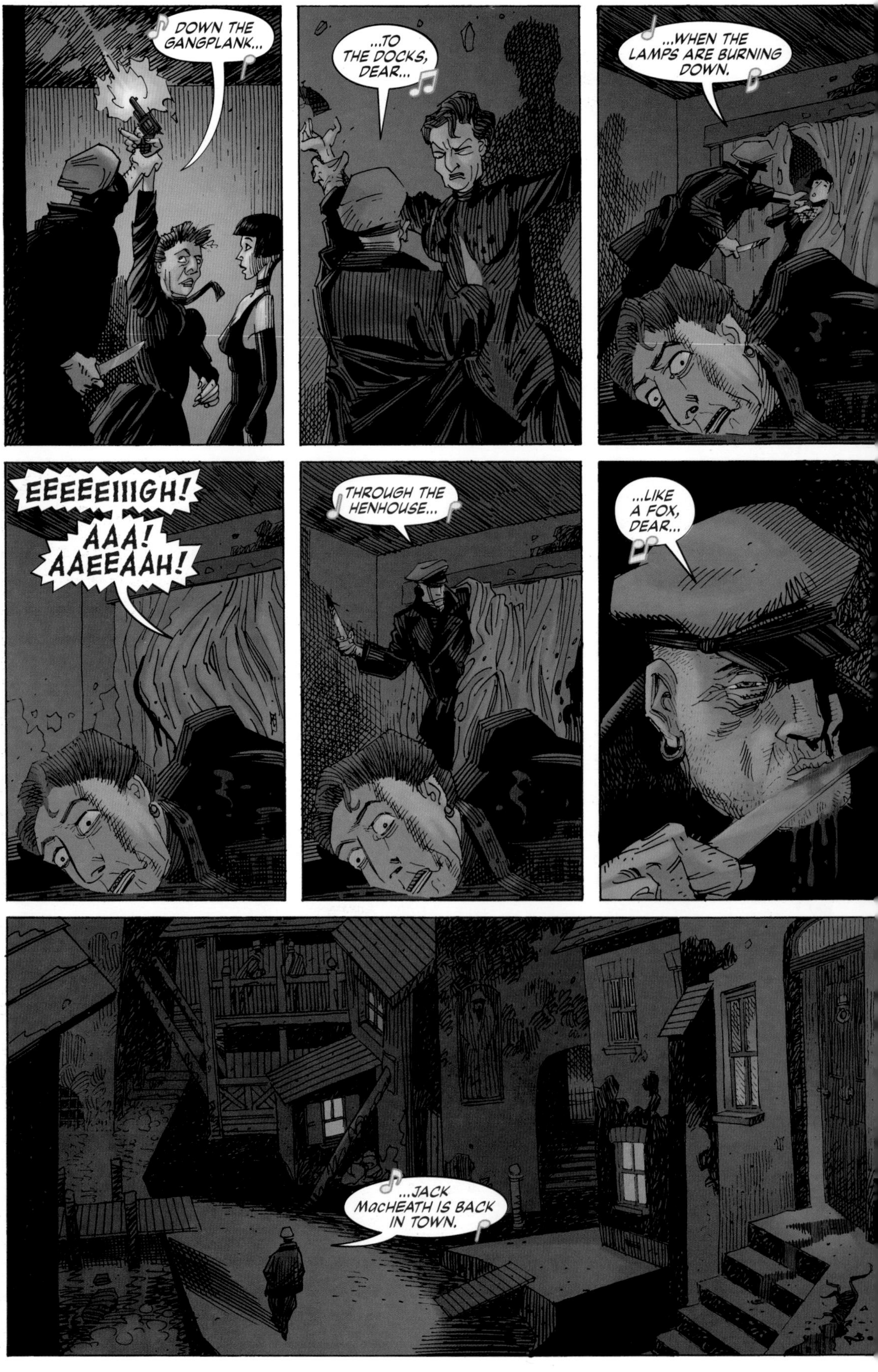
DOWN THE GANGPLANK...
...TO THE DOCKS, DEAR...
...WHEN THE LAMPS ARE BURNING DOWN.
EEEEEIIIGH!
AAA! AAEEAAH!
THROUGH THE HENHOUSE...
...LIKE A FOX, DEAR...
...JACK MacHEATH IS BACK IN TOWN.

You gentlemen can peek while she's slinging out the slops...

...and she's slinging out the slops as you're peeking.

Or you meet her in the hallway and you wink as you pass...

...and you make some smart remark about her titties or her arse...

...but you'll never know to whom you're speaking.

You have no IDEA to whom you are speaking.

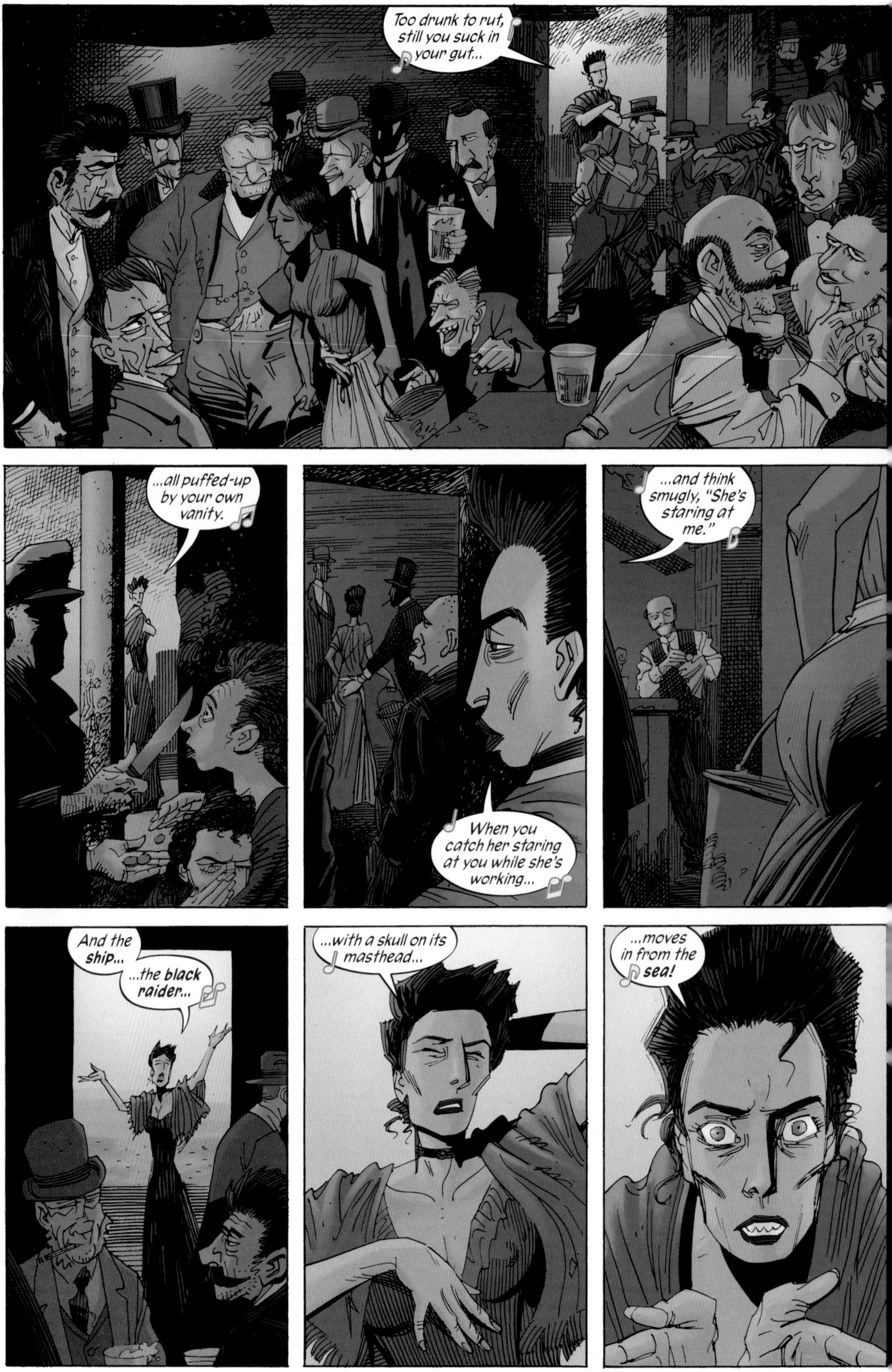
Too drunk to rut, still you suck in your gut...
...all puffed-up by your own vanity.
When you catch her staring at you while she's working...
...and think smugly, "She's staring at me."
And the ship...
...the black raider...
...with a skull on its masthead...
...moves in from the sea!

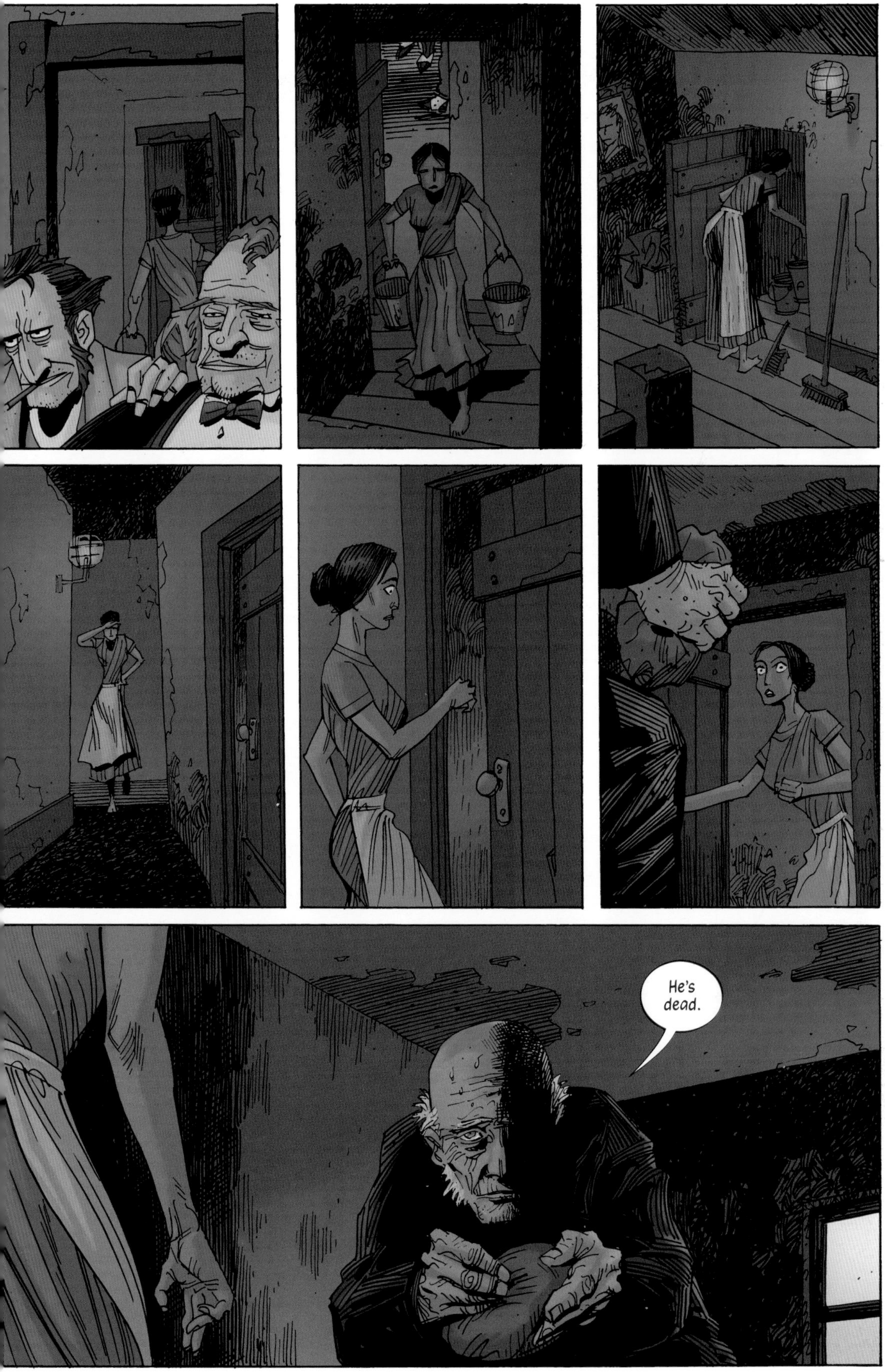

He's dead.

Hmm.

SO, BASICALLY, THEY'RE HOLDING A SÉANCE, THEN.

NO ENTRY

PRETTY MUCH.

MINA'S STILL WORRIED ABOUT THOSE OCCULTISTS IN CARNACKI'S VISION.

WELL, THE FOLDER I PINCHED SAID IFF KNOCKED AROUND WITH THAT SATANIST CHAP.

OLIVER HADDO. YES, IT SAID THEY'D BEEN CONNECTED.

BUT HADDO DIED TWO YEARS AGO, IN A FIRE...

YES, SUPPOSEDLY. IT'S A MURKY BUSINESS.

IT USUALLY IS WITH MINA.

COME ON. DO YOU FANCY STRETCHING YOUR LEGS?

I'LL SAY.

SHE WAS ORIGINALLY YOUR DAD'S COMPANION, WASN'T SHE?

Mm? Oh. Oh, Mina. Yes. Yes, she was.

WE THOUGHT WE'D KEEP HER IN THE FAMILY.

Ha. DON'T BLAME YOU.

WHAT ABOUT ORLANDO?

ORLANDO? WHAT DO YOU MEAN?

WELL, YOU KNOW. ALL THAT STUFF ABOUT POSING FOR THE MONA LISA AND WHAT-NOT.

IS HE BARMY?

DON'T LET HIM HEAR YOU SAY THAT.

WHETHER THAT'S SWORD'S EXCALIBUR OR NOT, HE'S AWFULLY GOOD WITH IT.

Is he... close to you two?

ALL DUE RESPECT, RAFFLES, THAT'S NONE OF YOUR BLOODY BUSINESS.

NO. NO, I SUPPOSE NOT. SORRY.

I'M JUST RATHER ON EDGE AT THE MOMENT.

Huh. CARNACKI'S DOOMSDAY PREDICTIONS GETTING TO YOU, ARE THEY?

IT'S NOT SO MUCH THAT.

I'M MORE WORRIED ABOUT THE PROSPECT OF A WAR.

WOULD YOU FIGHT?

I'D FEEL OBLIGED TO. I'VE BEEN A BIT OF A ROTTER OVER THE YEARS, QUATER-MAIN.

STILL, EVERYBODY DIES EVENTUALLY, EH?

Yes. YES, I SUPPOSE THEY DO.

WELL, MR. CARNACKI? ARE YOU GETTING ANY INFORMATION ABOUT IFF OR HADDO FROM YOUR... WHAT DID YOU CALL IT?

IT'S A SCRYING GLASS, A BLACK MIRROR MADE OF OBSIDIAN.

IT'S FROM THE MUSEUM'S COLLECTION. IT USED TO BELONG TO GLORIANA'S ALCHEMIST, JOHN SUBTLE.

OH, HONESTLY! SUBTLE WAS JUST A CODE-NAME THAT QUEEN GLORY GAVE TO DUKE PROSPERO OF MILAN. I WAS THERE.

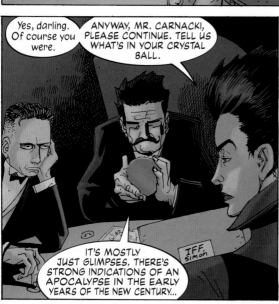

Yes, darling. Of course you were.

ANYWAY, MR. CARNACKI, PLEASE CONTINUE. TELL US WHAT'S IN YOUR CRYSTAL BALL.

IT'S MOSTLY JUST GLIMPSES. THERE'S STRONG INDICATIONS OF AN APOCALYPSE IN THE EARLY YEARS OF THE NEW CENTURY...

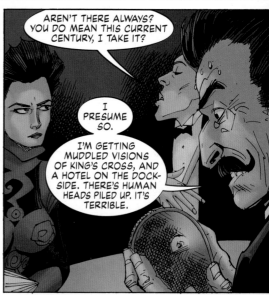

AREN'T THERE ALWAYS? YOU DO MEAN THIS CURRENT CENTURY, I TAKE IT?

I PRESUME SO.

I'M GETTING MUDDLED VISIONS OF KING'S CROSS, AND A HOTEL ON THE DOCK-SIDE. THERE'S HUMAN HEADS PILED UP. IT'S TERRIBLE.

I SEE. AND ARE SIMON IFF OR OLIVER HADDO INVOLVED IN ANY OF THIS?

YES. YES, I SENSE THEY'RE MIXED UP IN THE APOCALYPSE PART OF THE VISION.

I ALSO CONNECT THEM WITH KING'S CROSS.

"KING'S CROSS." THAT IS THE RAILWAY STATION, I SUPPOSE, AND NOT AN OBLIQUE REFERENCE TO THE IMMINENT CORONATION?

HM. I HADN'T THOUGHT OF THAT. THE WAY DIVINATION WORKS, IT COULD BE ALLUD-ING TO BOTH THINGS.

THAT SOUNDS OMINOUS.

WHAT ABOUT THIS HOTEL ON THE DOCKS YOU MENTIONED?

THAT'S MORE INDISTINCT.

I SENSE SOME THREAT...A RUTHLESS KILLER RECENTLY ARRIVED IN ENGLAND...SOME CRISIS ERUPTING ON CORONATION DAY. NOTHING SPECIFIC, THOUGH.

PERHAPS NOT... ALTHOUGH THE "RUTHLESS KILLER" PART INTRIGUES ME.

THE PAPERS REPORT SEVERAL DOCKSIDE PROSTITUTES MURDERED THESE LAST FEW WEEKS.

THERE'S EVEN SPECULATION THAT THE WHITECHAPEL FIEND HAS RETURNED...

...TO ASSASSINATE THE KING, NO DOUBT.

WELL, WHY NOT? IT'S SCARCELY MORE RIDICULOUS THAN YOU HAVING HIGH TEA WITH PROSPERO AND QUEEN GLORIANA.

OH, COME ON! IT'S A BIT ELABORATE, SURELY? AND WHERE DO THESE KING'S CROSS BLACK MAGICIANS FIT IN?

THEY MAY NOT FIT IN AT ALL. ON THE OTHER HAND, THEIR RITUALS MAY BE CAUSING ALL OF THESE EVENTS.

THANK YOU, MR. CARNACKI.

I PROPOSE WE INVESTIGATE KING'S CROSS...AFTER INFORMING MILITARY INTELLIGENCE, NATURALLY.

OH, BLAST! DOES THAT MEAN WE HAVE TO SIT THROUGH A MEETING WITH FATTY HOLMES?

WELL, NOT ALL OF US, SURELY?

BESIDES, HOLMES MIGHT HAVE USEFUL INFORMATION. ONE MEETING'S HARDLY THE END OF THE WORLD.

Hm.

YES, WELL.

LET'S HOPE NOT, ANYWAY.

I...I DIDN'T THINK HE'D EVER REALLY DIE.

I DON'T KNOW HOW I FEEL. WE DIDN'T EVEN LIKE EACH OTHER...

THAT'S NOT TRUE.

BLESS YOU, MISS, YOU WERE ALL HE LIVED FOR.

WHEN YOU RUN OFF, HIS HEART BROKE.

HE WANTED A SUCCESSOR, ISHMAEL. NOT A DAUGHTER.

Aye, well...

TO TELL THE TRUTH, MISS JANNI, THAT WAS ONE OF THE THINGS I'D COME HERE TO TALK TO YOU ABOUT.

WHAT?

ISHMAEL, HOW *COULD* YOU? YOU KNOW I'LL NEVER AGREE. IT WAS WHY I RAN AWAY IN THE FIRST PLACE...

HEAR ME OUT, MISS...

IT WAS HIS DYING WISH. HE ASKED ME TO...TO MAKE SOME CHANGES TO THE NAUTILUS, THEN GIVE IT TO YOU.

NO, ISHMAEL!

I DON'T WANT IT! I DON'T WANT TO BE A FANATIC!

ANYWAY, I'VE MADE A NEW LIFE HERE...

NOT MUCH OF ONE, THOUGH.

YOU...YOU CAN'T SAY THAT. I'M... I'M GETTING ON WELL. I'M RESPECTED.

RESPECTED?

JANNI, YOU COULD BE OUR *QUEEN*. JUST SAY THE WORD, LASS.

Ishmael, I'm not...

MISS JANNI. I'M BEGGING YOU. I NEED A CAPTAIN, MISS. WE ALL DO.

LOOK, AT LEAST TAKE THIS FLARE GUN.

FLARE GUN...?

FOR IF YOU CHANGE YOUR MIND. THE NAUTILUS IS MOORED IN THE THAMES ESTUARY.

IF YOU EVER WANT US, MISS, JUST...

NO! HAVEN'T YOU BEEN LISTENING TO ME?

GET OUT, ISHMAEL! GET OUT AND LEAVE ME ALONE!

M-MISS, JANNI, PLEASE...

ISHMAEL, JUST *GO!*

I WON'T CHANGE MY MIND. YOU *KNOW* THAT, IF YOU KNOW ANYTHING ABOUT ME.

AYE, MISS. I RECKON I DO.

YOU'RE STUBBORN.

JUST LIKE YOUR FATHER.

NO VISITORS
SPITTING
DRINK
DOGS

More tea?

Yes. Yes, thank you, we will.

Splendid. Bond? More tea for our guests, if you would.

Does...does madam require milk with her tea?

Oh, yes please. Just a splash would be lovely.

So, to business. What of Carnacki's visions?

Well, they're imprecise, but partly they concern a murderer, recently arrived on London's docksides.

Hmm. Yes, the MacHeath case.

We're already studying that.

MacHeath?

John MacHeath, a merchant navy captain recently returned from Argentina.

He left England in 1888, the year of the Whitechapel slayings.

Bloody hell.

Well, quite.

He's also a direct descendant of MacHeath the 18th century highway-man.

A police inspector, "Tiger" Brown, is currently looking into it.

I see.

Actually, Mr. Carnacki thought one occult source might be behind ALL of these events.

This would be the sect you mentioned?

YES. THE HADDO CULT. OUR ASSOCIATE MR. RAFFLES ACQUIRED INFORMATION LINKING A SUSPECT OF OURS WITH HADDO.

WELL, OF COURSE, MR. HADDO IS OFFICIALLY DEAD...

...ALTHOUGH HIS MAGICAL ORDER HAS SURVIVED HIM.

I THINK THEIR "PROFESS-HOUSE" OR WHATEVER IT'S CALLED IS NEAR KING'S CROSS.

Really? THAT'S INTERESTING.

KING'S CROSS FEATURED IN CARNACKI'S VISIONS. DO WE HAVE YOUR LEAVE TO INVESTIGATE?

I SUPPOSE SO.

YOU SHOULD CONSULT MR. NORTON FIRST, THOUGH.

NORTON? YOU MEAN ANDREW NORTON, THE PRISONER OF LONDON?

YES. HE'S GOOD WITH THE OCCULT STUFF AND DUE TO MATERIALIZE AT KING'S CROSS SOON, APPARENTLY.

BESIDES, I BELIEVE HE WORKED WITH YOUR PREDECESSORS.

INCIDENTALLY, HOW WAS MY BROTHER WHEN YOU VISITED HIM LAST?

HE'S WELL.

H-He sends regards.

Haha! MY DEAR MISS MURRAY AND MR. QUATERMAIN... JUNIOR.

IT'S ALWAYS A PLEASURE, EVEN WHEN I KNOW YOU'RE LYING.

PLEASE, SHOW YOUR-SELVES OUT.

CUTTLEFISH HOTEL

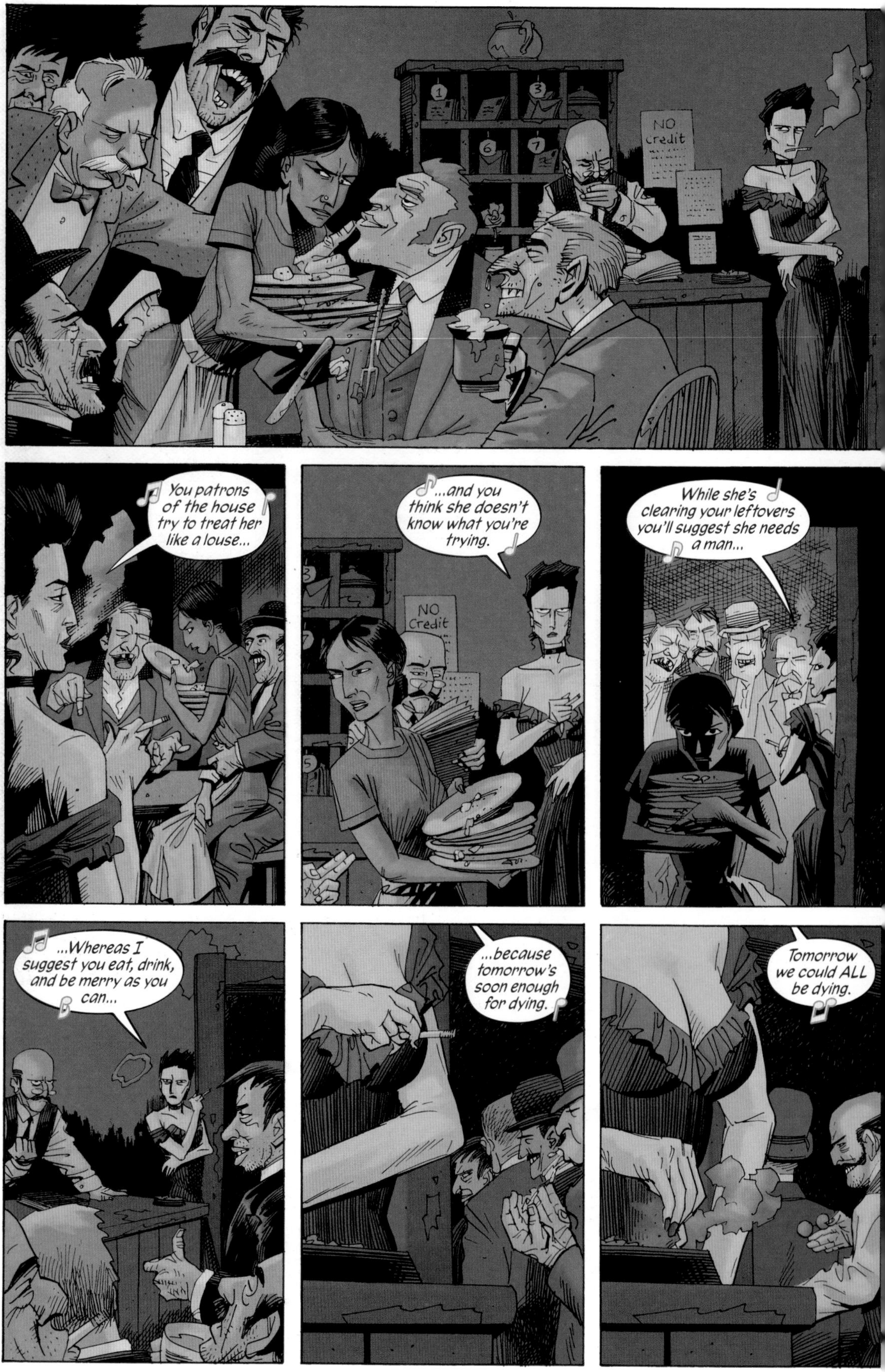
NO credit
You patrons of the house try to treat her like a louse...
...and you think she doesn't know what you're trying.
NO Credit
While she's clearing your leftovers you'll suggest she needs a man...
...Whereas I suggest you eat, drink, and be merry as you can...
...because tomorrow's soon enough for dying.
Tomorrow we could ALL be dying.

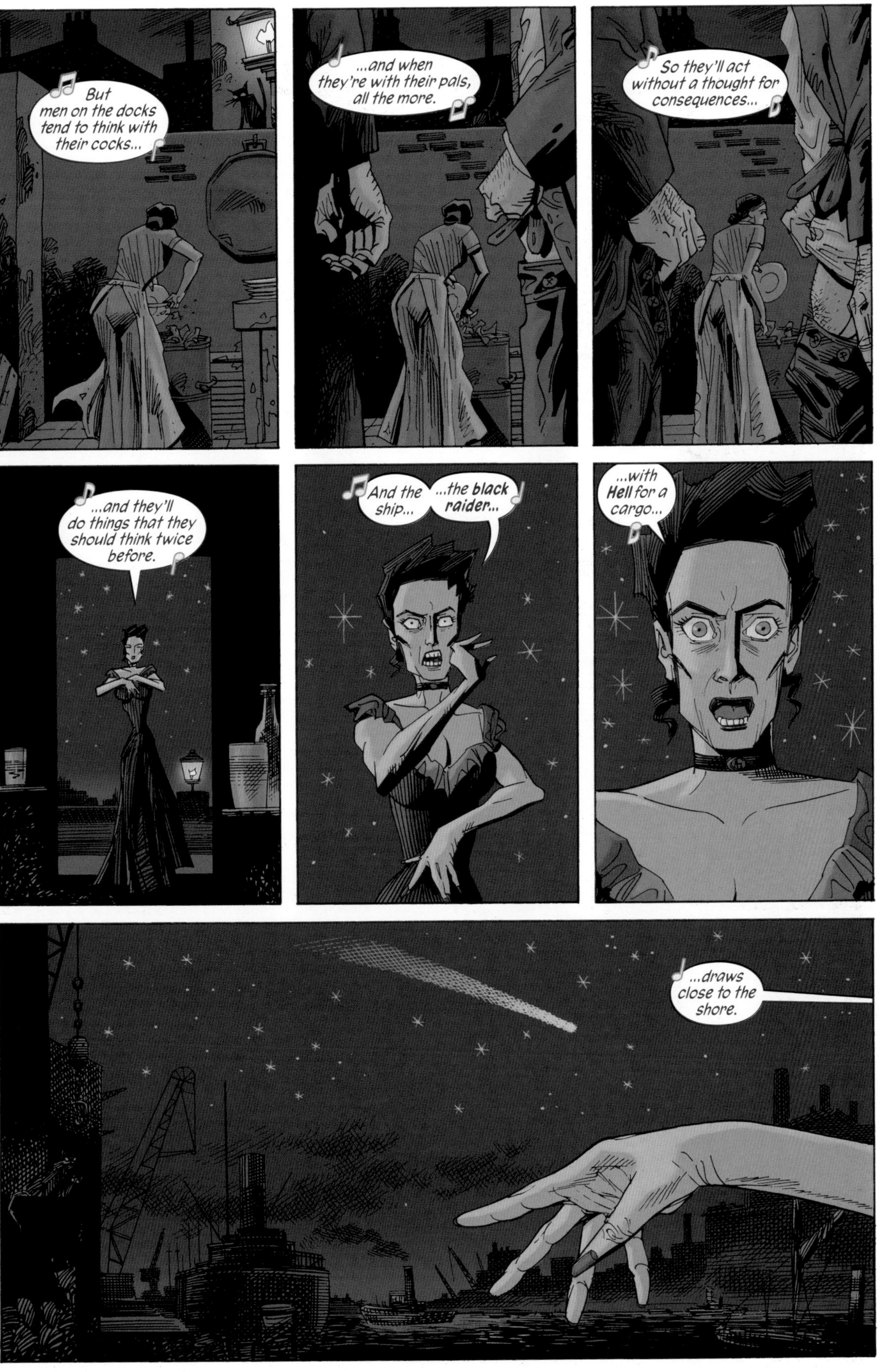

But men on the docks tend to think with their cocks...
...and when they're with their pals, all the more.
So they'll act without a thought for consequences...
...and they'll do things that they should think twice before.
And the ship...
...the **black raider**...
...with **Hell** for a cargo...
...draws close to the shore.

SO... ...WHO'S THIS NORTON?

NORTON? I'M AFRAID I HAVEN'T MET HIM BEFORE. I'VE ONLY HEARD ABOUT HIM.

I'M TOLD I'LL KNOW HIM WHEN I SEE HIM. HE WORKED WITH THE 17th AND 18th CENTURY VERSIONS OF THIS GROUP, APPARENTLY.

OH, GOD. NOT ANOTHER "IMMORTAL" LIKE ORLANDO?

NO. NO, MR. NORTON'S REPUTEDLY MORE COMPLICATED THAN THAT.

THEY CALL HIM "THE PRISONER OF LONDON." HE'S CONFINED TO THIS CITY, BUT NOT TO ANY ONE CENTURY.

ORLANDO'S ENCOUNTERED HIM ONCE OR TWICE, OR SO HE CLAIMS.

WHY ISN'T ORLANDO HERE, THEN?

WELL, FIRSTLY, WHEN ORLANDO'S MALE HE RATHER IRRITATES ME.

SECONDLY, HE'S MORE USEFUL WITH ALLAN AND CARNACKI, INVESTIGATING THIS NEARBY CULT HEADQUARTERS, SO...HANG ON.

CAN YOU FEEL THAT PRESSURE IN YOUR EARS?

I THINK IT MEANS NORTON'S ALMOST HERE...

£50 REWARD
GEORGE M PLUMMER

the BEAST
NEW RIPPER HORRORS
SCOTLAND YARD IS

Blimey.

M-MINA, IS THIS GOING TO BE ALL RIGHT? MY HAIR'S STANDING UP ON END...

I...I DON'T KNOW. I HAVEN'T FELT ANYTHING REMOTELY LIKE THIS SINCE ALLAN AND I WERE IN ARKHAM.

TH-THIS SENSATION THAT SOMETHING IS JUST ABOUT TO...

...break through...

HI. How are you?

Um..."hi." W-WE'RE VERY WELL, THANK YOU.

Y-YOU MUST BE ANDREW NORTON. THIS IS ANTHONY RAFFLES AND I'M MINA MURRAY.

GASLIGHT UNDER-STUDIES.

MARVELLOUS.

UH... YOU KNOW OF US, THEN?

OF COURSE. COFFINS AT CARFAX, BLOOD FOR OIL. PATRICK KEILLER MAPPING THE MARTIANS' CRATER.

DEAD TRAILS. ABANDONED PANICS.

I...I SEE.

ACTUALLY, MR. NORTON, WE WERE HOPING YOU COULD INFORM US CONCERNING ONE OLIVER HADDO, AND ALSO CERTAIN ACTIVITIES CENTRED ON KING'S CROSS...

HADDO? CROWLEY MANQUÉ. THE GREAT BEAST REFLECTED IN AN OVER-POLISHED OCCASIONAL TABLE. KING'S CROSS, THOUGH... I'D ADVISE YOU TO BE CAREFUL.

THE PLACE IS A MYTH-SUMP, INVITES APOCALYPTIC THINKING. DANGEROUS AGENDAS HURRYING TO MAKE THEIR CONNECTION.

APOCALYPTIC? HOW DO YOU MEAN?

ISN'T IT OBVIOUS? JULY SEVENTH. PARADISE BACKPACKERS.

A CONSTELLATION OF CIGARETTE BURNS ON ARCHER'S BACK. THE STARS ARE RIGHT.

MISPLACED MEMORIALS. FOR-GOTTEN FIRES. RIMBAUD, VERLAINE, LYRIC GREASE. BOADICEA'S URBAN LEGEND UNDER PLATFORM TEN.

A QUARTER PLATFORM OVER, THE FRANCHISE EXPRESS, GATHERING STEAM.

Anyway...

I'M AFRAID I CAN'T STAY. APPOINTMENTS UP THE ROAD: MAGIC REVIVALS, HYDE PARK HAPPENINGS, DAVID LITVINOV'S VENTRILOQUISM, JACK THE HAT.

I EXPECT I'LL SEE YOU IN 1969.

WHAT? MR. NORTON, YOU HAVEN'T ANSWERED OUR QUESTIONS! DON'T...

MINA, COME AWAY. SOMETHING'S HAPPENING...

HE'S...HE'S GONE.

A.J., I DIDN'T UNDERSTAND ANY OF THAT. WHO'S ARCHER? WHO'S LITVINOV?

D-DO YOU KNOW, FOR THE FIRST TIME IN MY LIFE, I FEEL STUPID...

THE FELLOW TALKED IN BLOODY CROSSWOOD CLUES! HE DID LINK KING'S CROSS WITH APOCALYPSE, THOUGH...

...WITH POTENTIALLY WORLD-ENDING CONSEQUENCES, IF NORTON'S RIGHT.

I MEAN, A BAD ENOUGH MISTAKE COULD SPELL ABSOLUTE DISASTER.

YES. YES, HE DID.

COME ON, A.J. OUR COLLEAGUES ARE SUPPOSEDLY ONLY ON SUR-VEILLANCE, BUT IN ORLANDO'S PRESENT MOOD HE MIGHT DO SOMETHING RASH...

It must have got you hard when you had her in the yard...

...but you've no idea how hard things are getting.

And you think of what you've done as you're buttoning your flies...

Of an act so bloody shameful you can't look me in the eyes...

...and which you imagine you're regretting.

Believe me, you don't **KNOW** regretting.

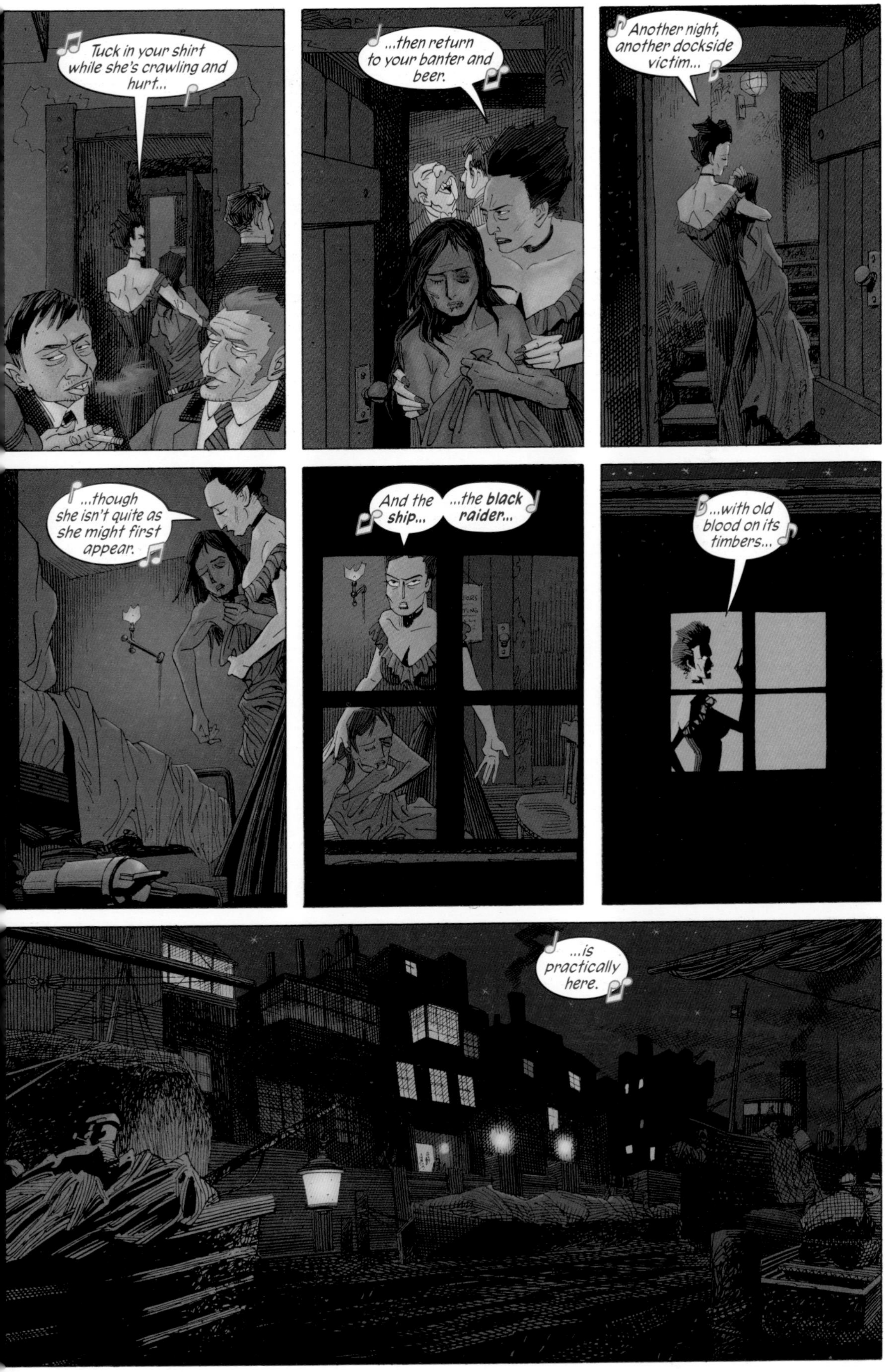
Tuck in your shirt while she's crawling and hurt...
...then return to your banter and beer.
Another night, another dockside victim...
...though she isn't quite as she might first appear.
And the ship...
...the black raider...
...with old blood on its timbers...
...is practically here.

ORLANDO, MISS MURRAY SAID WE SHOULD OBSERVE THIS PLACE, NOT BREAK IN.

YES, WELL. FRANKLY, CARNACKI, MINA CAN SOMETIMES BE RATHER UN-ADVENTUROUS.

I'LL TELL HER YOU SAID THAT, AND YOU'LL BE LOSING YOUR BALLS EARLIER THAN YOU EXPECTED.

OH, COME ON, ALLAN. WHERE'S THE HARM?

I MEAN, RAFFLES IS *ALWAYS* BREAKING AND ENTERING. SHE DOESN'T MIND *HIM*.

Hm. D'YOU THINK HE FANCIES HER?

LOOK, CAN WE JUST *DO* THIS?

ALL RIGHT, CARNACKI, DON'T GET IN A FUNK.

I'M NO RAFFLES, EVIDENTLY, BUT I WAS ONCE *VERY* CLOSE TO SINBAD.

PEGO LIKE A STALLION'S...

...AND THE MOST INGENIOUS THIEF OF THE EIGHTH CENTURY.

Ah.

THERE WE GO.

I--I CAN'T SAY I LIKE THE ATMOSPHERE.

HE'S GOT A POINT, LANDO. IF I'D KNOWN WE WERE BREAKING IN I'D HAVE BROUGHT A GUN.

OH, DO DRY UP, THE PAIR OF YOU.

WHO NEEDS GUNS WHEN I'M HERE WITH MY FABLED BLADE?

LANDO, THAT SWORD ISN'T EXCALIBUR.

YES IT *IS*. AND I HAD TO SUBDUE THE *REAL* LADY OF THE LAKE...A TERRIFYING UNDINE...IN ORDER TO GRAB IT.

FELLOWS, PLEASE...

I THINK YOU SHOULD BE TAKING THIS MORE SERIOUSLY.

WHAT IF OLIVER HADDO REALLY IS STILL ALIVE?

SURELY, HADDO WAS JUST A FRAUD?

OF COURSE HE WAS.

BELIEVE ME, DEAR, AFTER YOU'VE KNOWN MERLIN, FAUST AND PROSPERO, THEY'RE *ALL* FRAUDS.

YES, WELL. LET'S HOPE YOU'RE RIGHT.

OF COURSE I'M RIGHT.

MODERN OCCULTISTS ARE ALL TALK.

PROSPERO HAD MORE POWER IN HIS LITTLE FINGER THAN THEY'VE GOT IN THEIR...

...entire...

Gentlemen...

...WON'T YOU COME IN?

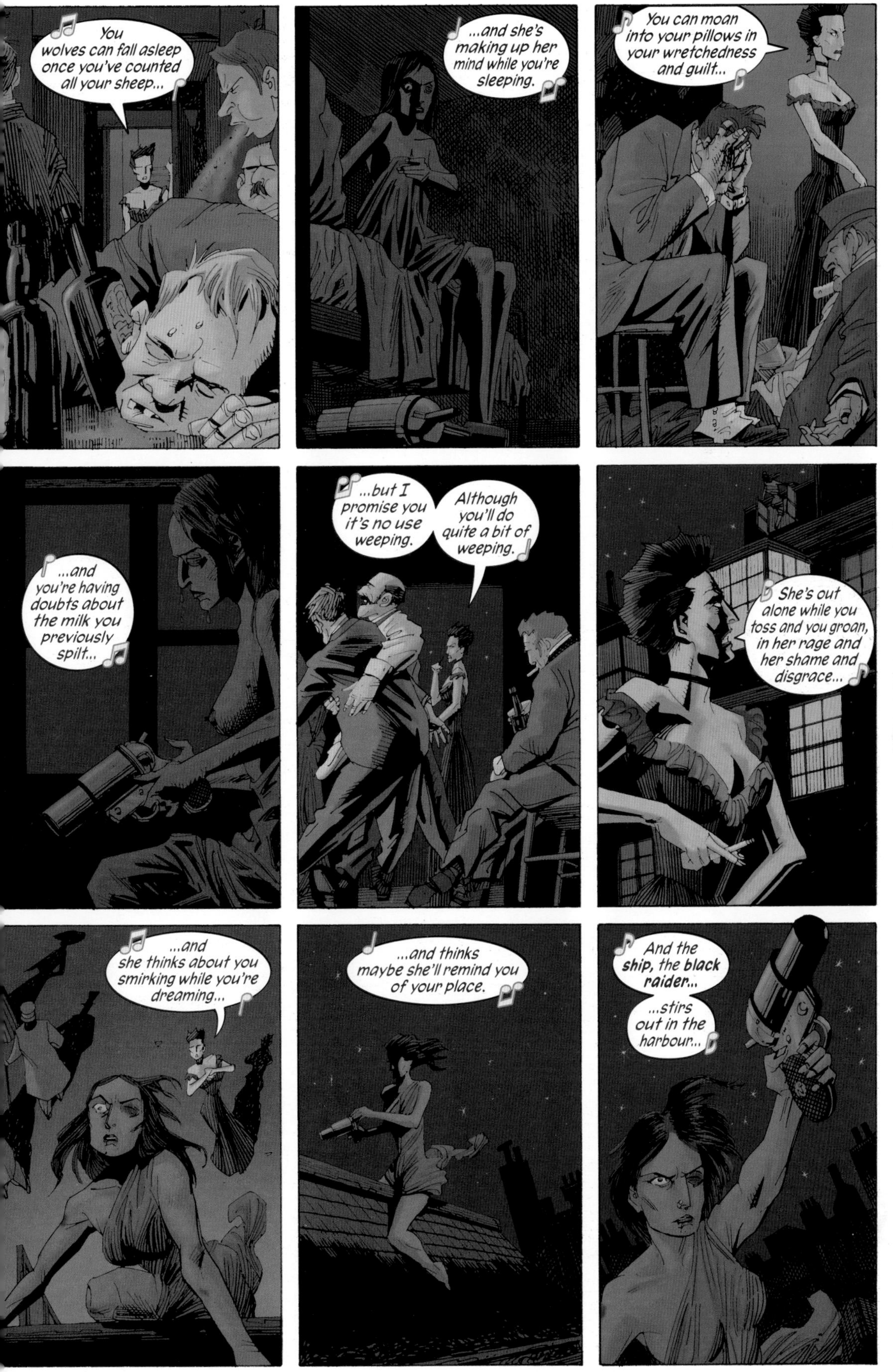
You wolves can fall asleep once you've counted all your sheep...
...and she's making up her mind while you're sleeping.
You can moan into your pillows in your wretchedness and guilt...
...and you're having doubts about the milk you previously spilt...
...but I promise you it's no use weeping.
Although you'll do quite a bit of weeping.
She's out alone while you toss and you groan, in her rage and her shame and disgrace...
...and she thinks about you smirking while you're dreaming...
...and thinks maybe she'll remind you of your place.
And the **ship, the black raider...**
...stirs out in the harbour...

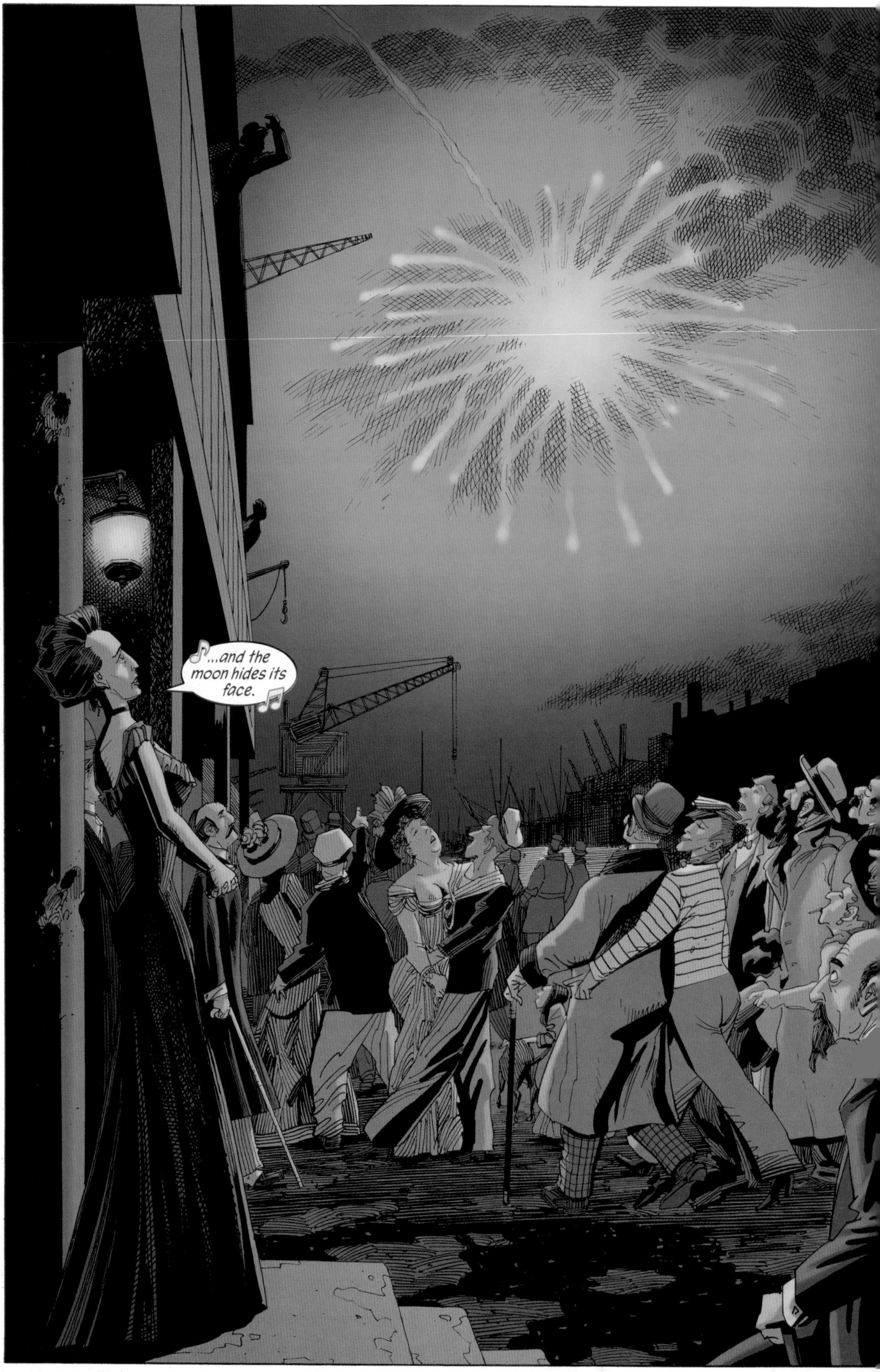
♪...and the moon hides its face.♫

GOOD GOD.

MINA, LOOK AT THAT.

IT LOOKS LIKE IT'S OVER THE EAST END.

YES. YES, IT DOES. LET'S ASK THIS BOBBY IF HE KNOWS ANYTHING.

CONSTABLE? EXCUSE ME...

I'M WILHELMINA MURRAY. WE'RE WITH MILITARY INTELLIGENCE. DO YOU KNOW WHAT THAT FLARE IS IN AID OF?

WELL, MISS, THEY'VE POSSIBLY CAPTURED MacHEATH.

MacHEATH THE DOCKSIDE MURDERER?

THAT'S HIM. IF TIGER BROWN'S COLLARED MacHEATH, THAT FLARE COULD BE THE TARTS CELE-BRATING.

I HEAR HE'LL HANG BEFORE DAWN.

BEFORE DAWN? THAT'S A BIT HASTY, ISN'T IT?

IT'S WHAT YOUR INTELLIGENCE PEOPLE ORDERED, I'M TOLD.

ANYWAY, I'D BEST BE GETTING ON.

EVENING, ALL.

MINA, IS THERE SOMETHING GOING ON HERE THAT WE'RE MISSING?

VERY POSSIBLY.

COME ON. LET'S RECALL ALLAN AND THE OTHERS FROM THEIR SURVEILLANCE MISSION...

...BEFORE WE GET IN DEEPER OVER OUR HEADS THAN WE ALREADY ARE.

WHAT HAVE YOU DONE TO TO HIM? HE'S BARELY BREATHING.

Hm. THAT *IS* UNUSUAL. AFTER MY BLASTING ROD, THEY'RE GENERALLY NOT BREATHING AT ALL.

ANYWAY, THE QUESTION IS, WHO ARE YOU? WHAT ARE YOU DOING HERE?

I KNOW THE OLDER FELLOW FROM MY CLUB, MASTER. HE'S CARNACKI. CARNACKI THE GHOST FINDER.

OH...THE WHISTLING ROOM CAPER? I'VE HEARD OF YOU.

AND I OF YOU.

YOU ARE OLIVER HADDO, I TAKE IT?

WHAT? ME? OF COURSE NOT. HADDO'S DEAD. HADN'T YOU HEARD?

I'M DR. KARSWELL TRELAWNEY, VARIOUSLY OF STONEDENE, AND LUFFORD IN WARWICKSHIRE.

FRATER SIMON YOU APPARENTLY KNOW ALREADY. THIS IS SOROR CYBELE, AND THERE'S FRATER CYRIL.

YES. YES, IT'S EXACTLY AS IT WAS IN MY DREAM, EXCEPT...

EXCEPT THERE WAS ANOTHER WOMAN. SOME-ONE CALLED "ILIEL."

NEVER HEARD OF HER.

ILIEL, THOUGH... THE NAME ADDS UP TO EIGHTY-ONE. A LUNAR NUMBER.

LUNAR...I REMEMBER NOW. IN MY DREAM YOU WERE PLANNING TO CREATE SOMETHING CALLED A MOONCHILD...

REALLY? WELL, DREAMS CAN BE NONSENSE. I ASSURE YOU, I'VE CURRENTLY NO SUCH PLAN.

WE ARE SIMPLE OCCULT SCHOLARS.

THE MASTER'S RIGHT. WE MERELY REPRESENT AN INVISIBLE COLLEGE.

ABSOLUTELY. WE'RE RATHER LIKE THE ROSICRUCIANS. WE GATHER IN OUR "HOUSE OF PROFESSORS" TO WORSHIP.

SO, MR. CARNACKI, PERHAPS YOUR PORTENTOUS VISIONS WERE MISTAKEN?

ON THE OTHER HAND, IT'S CONCEIVABLE THAT THEY SIMPLY HAVEN'T HAPPENED YET.

NOW, PERHAPS YOU'D TAKE YOUR DISHY YOUNG FRIEND AND LEAVE...

...BEFORE HE FINDS HIMSELF ON THE WRONG END OF MY *OTHER* BLASTING ROD.

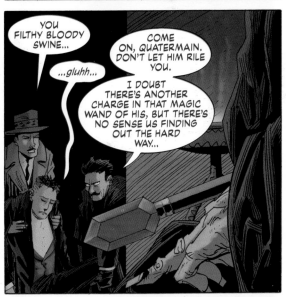

YOU FILTHY BLOODY SWINE...

...gluhh...

COME ON, QUATERMAIN. DON'T LET HIM RILE YOU.

I DOUBT THERE'S ANOTHER CHARGE IN THAT MAGIC WAND OF HIS, BUT THERE'S NO SENSE US FINDING OUT THE HARD WAY...

WELL, NOW, FRATER CYRIL. THERE'S A SIGN FROM THE GODS IF EVER I SAW ONE.

EVIDENTLY WE SHOULD LOCATE SOMEONE TO BE THIS "SOROR ILIEL"...

...AND ONLY *THEN* SHOULD WE COMMENCE OUR MOONCHILD.

oh, FOR GOD'S SAKE!

WHAT THE BLOODY HELL HAPPENED TO HIM?

he...HE WAS BLASTED WITH HADDO'S WAND.

w-WE'RE PRETTY SURE IT WAS HADDO...

HADDO? WHAT WERE YOU DOING CONFRONTING HADDO, YOU IDIOTS?

YOU WERE SUPPOSED TO BE ON A SURVEILLANCE MISSION!

WELL, YOU SEE, ORLANDO SAID...

ORLANDO? AND DO YOU TAKE INSTRUCTIONS FROM THIS...THIS DELUSIONAL TROLLOP, OR FROM ME?

m-MINA, DEAR HEART, I AM ACTUALLY PRESENT, YOU KNOW.

I DON'T CARE! THIS GROUP IS A SHAMBLES!

DARE I ASK IF YOU LEARNED ANYTHING VALUABLE?

COME ON, DARLING. WE DID OUR BEST...

DON'T "DARLING" ME. AND I TAKE IT THE ANSWER TO MY QUESTION IS "NO?"

th-THE CULT AREN'T PLANNING ANYTHING. I-IT WASN'T LIKE MY DREAM...

I SEE. SO ALL THIS HAS BEEN POINTLESS.

AND THAT'S OUR FAULT, IS IT? WHAT ABOUT YOU?

DID THIS NORTON TELL YOU ANY-THING?

TH-THAT ISN'T THE ISSUE.

AT LEAST WE LEARNED MACHEATH IS TO BE HUNG AT DAWN TOMORROW.

WHAT? HOLMES DIDN'T TELL US ABOUT THAT...

NO, HE DIDN'T. I SUGGEST WE LOCATE THE PROPOSED EXECUTION SITE AND FIND OUT WHY.

THIS TEAM'S USELESS. WE NEED TO GET A *GRIP* ON THINGS.

Mm.

WELL, PERHAPS IF WE HAD BETTER *LEADERSHIP* WE MIGHT NOT SPEND OUR TIME RUNNING IN CIRCLES.

NOW, WHEN I WAS *ALEXANDER'S* ADVISOR...

OH! THAT IS THE ABSOLUTE *LIMIT!*

LISTEN, YOU CAN HAVE THE DOUBLE BED TO *YOURSELVES* TONIGHT. I'M SLEEPING DOWNSTAIRS.

Mina! Don't tell the neighbourhood...

OH, SHUT UP! I'LL BE AT MACHEATH'S EXECUTION.

UNLESS YOUR NEW *STRATEGIST* CONCOCTS A *BETTER* PLAN, I EXPECT I'LL SEE YOU THERE.

MINA...

WELL, THAT'S TORN IT.

LANDO, THAT HAS TO BE THE MOST STUPID THING YOU'VE EVER SAID.

OH, I DON'T KNOW. THERE WAS, "OH LOOK! WHAT A WONDERFUL HORSE!"

THAT WAS AT TROY.

♪ As morning gently breaks, all you libertines and rakes can congratulate yourselves on your fast one. ♪♪

When she walks into the lobby ♪ you look hurriedly away...

♪ ...and pretend to be concerned about the matters of the day... ♪

♪ ...as engrossed as if it were your last one. ♪

We never know which one's our last one.

She sits there calm while outside there's alarm, and you have your first moment of doubt...

...when you notice that she's smiling through her bruises...

♪ ...and you think, "Christ, what's **she** got to smile about?" ♪

♪ ...and the **ship**, the **black raider**, is announced on the wharfside...

♪ ...by a scream from without.

LEFISH HOTEL

MR. HOLMES, THERE YOU ARE.

WOULD YOU MIND TELLING ME WHAT'S GOING ON?

NOT AT ALL. IT'S AN EXECUTION. WE'RE HANGING MacHEATH.

WITH RESPECT, SIR, I KNOW THAT. BUT WHY SO HURRIEDLY? IS THERE TO BE NO TRIAL?

OF COURSE NOT. IT MIGHT EMBARRASS THE ARISTOCRACY.

THE ARISTOCRACY? WHAT DO THEY HAVE TO DO WITH ANYTHING?

MY DEAR LADY, THIS IS ENGLAND. THEY HAVE TO DO WITH EVERYTHING...

...ESPECIALLY 1888'S NOTORIOUS WHITECHAPEL MURDERS.

YOU SEE, MacHEATH ABSCONDED FOR ARGENTINA IN EARLY DECEMBER THAT YEAR.

THE LAST MURDER HAPPENED ON BOXING DAY.

M-MacHEATH DIDN'T DO THE LAST ONE? SO WHO...?

THE PROSTITUTE'S NAME WAS GRACE.

WE BELIEVE SHE WAS DISEMBOWELED BY THE 14TH EARL OF GURNEY.

BETTER EVERYONE THINKS MacHEATH DID THEM ALL, eh? A TRIAL WOULD ONLY RAISE AWKWARD QUESTIONS.

INCIDENTALLY, HOW DID YOUR PREDICTED ARMAGEDDON TURN OUT?

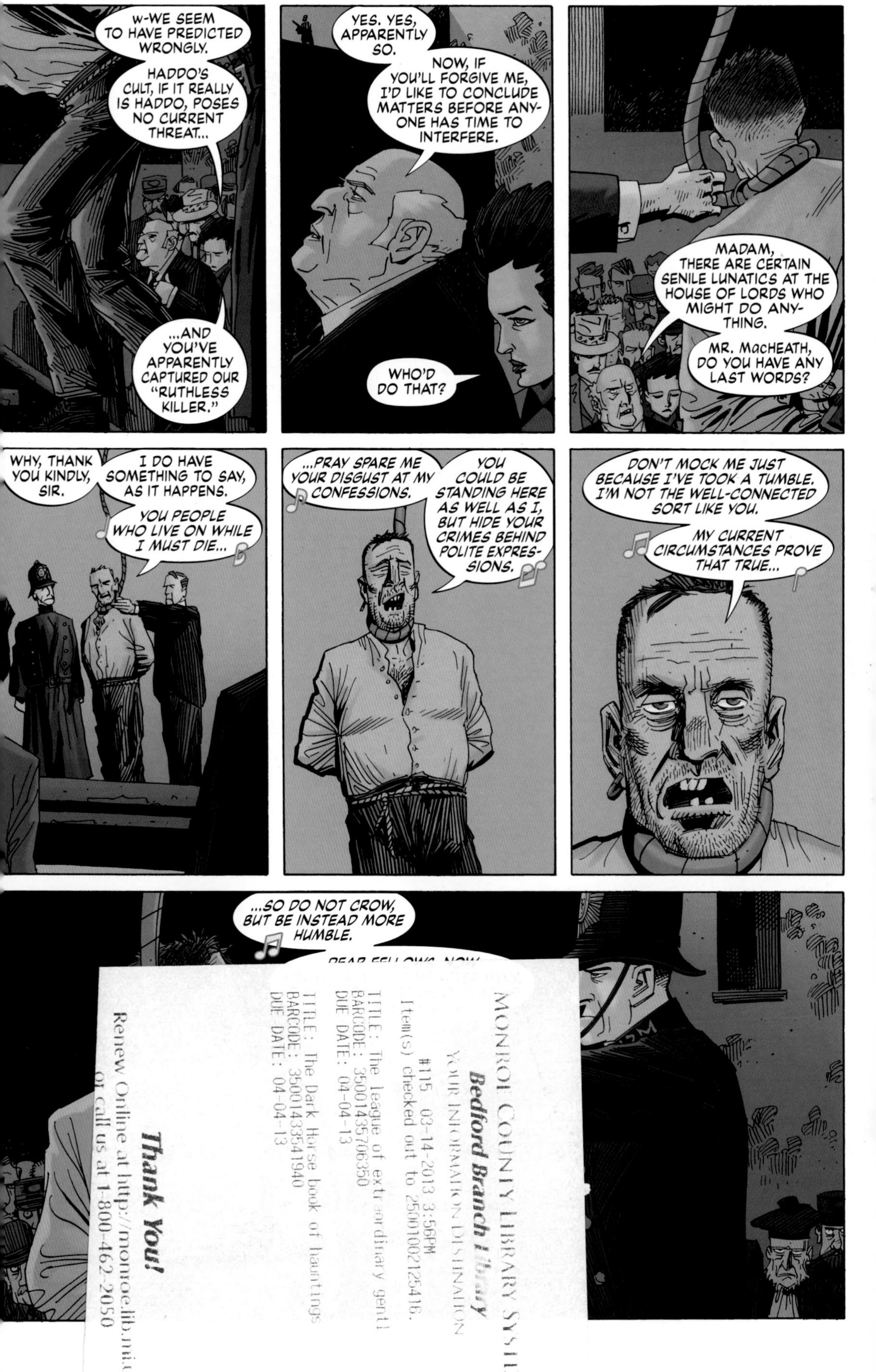
W-WE SEEM TO HAVE PREDICTED WRONGLY.
HADDO'S CULT, IF IT REALLY IS HADDO, POSES NO CURRENT THREAT...
...AND YOU'VE APPARENTLY CAPTURED OUR "RUTHLESS KILLER."
YES. YES, APPARENTLY SO.
NOW, IF YOU'LL FORGIVE ME, I'D LIKE TO CONCLUDE MATTERS BEFORE ANY-ONE HAS TIME TO INTERFERE.
WHO'D DO THAT?
MADAM, THERE ARE CERTAIN SENILE LUNATICS AT THE HOUSE OF LORDS WHO MIGHT DO ANY-THING.
MR. MacHEATH, DO YOU HAVE ANY LAST WORDS?
WHY, THANK YOU KINDLY, SIR.
I DO HAVE SOMETHING TO SAY, AS IT HAPPENS.
YOU PEOPLE WHO LIVE ON WHILE I MUST DIE...
...PRAY SPARE ME YOUR DISGUST AT MY CONFESSIONS.
YOU COULD BE STANDING HERE AS WELL AS I, BUT HIDE YOUR CRIMES BEHIND POLITE EXPRES-SIONS.
DON'T MOCK ME JUST BECAUSE I'VE TOOK A TUMBLE. I'M NOT THE WELL-CONNECTED SORT LIKE YOU.
MY CURRENT CIRCUMSTANCES PROVE THAT TRUE...
...SO DO NOT CROW, BUT BE INSTEAD MORE HUMBLE.

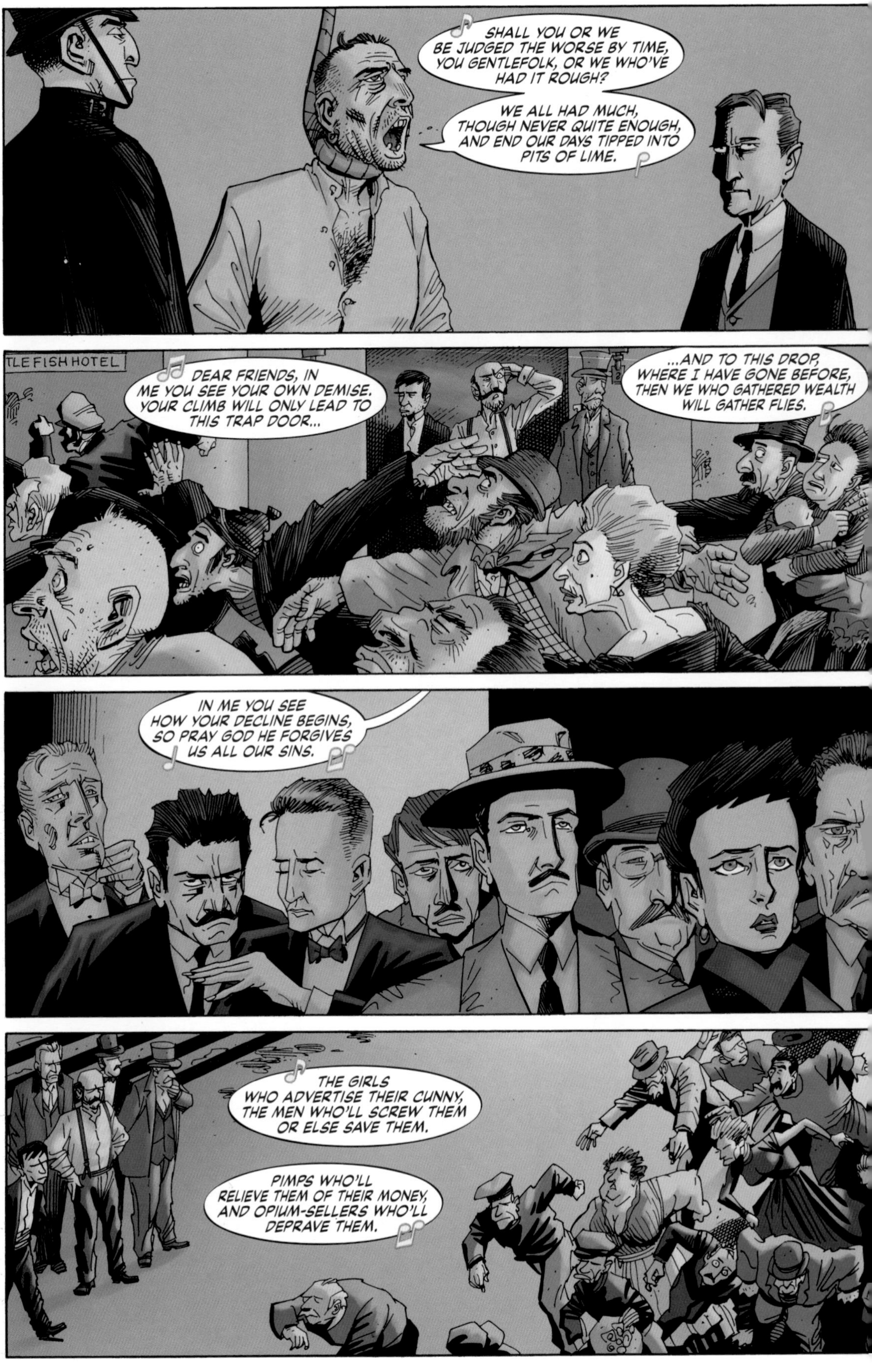
SHALL YOU OR WE BE JUDGED THE WORSE BY TIME, YOU GENTLEFOLK, OR WE WHO'VE HAD IT ROUGH?
WE ALL HAD MUCH, THOUGH NEVER QUITE ENOUGH, AND END OUR DAYS TIPPED INTO PITS OF LIME.
TLE FISH HOTEL
DEAR FRIENDS, IN ME YOU SEE YOUR OWN DEMISE. YOUR CLIMB WILL ONLY LEAD TO THIS TRAP DOOR...
...AND TO THIS DROP, WHERE I HAVE GONE BEFORE, THEN WE WHO GATHERED WEALTH WILL GATHER FLIES.
IN ME YOU SEE HOW YOUR DECLINE BEGINS, SO PRAY GOD HE FORGIVES US ALL OUR SINS.
THE GIRLS WHO ADVERTISE THEIR CUNNY, THE MEN WHO'LL SCREW THEM OR ELSE SAVE THEM.
PIMPS WHO'LL RELIEVE THEM OF THEIR MONEY, AND OPIUM-SELLERS WHO'LL DEPRAVE THEM.

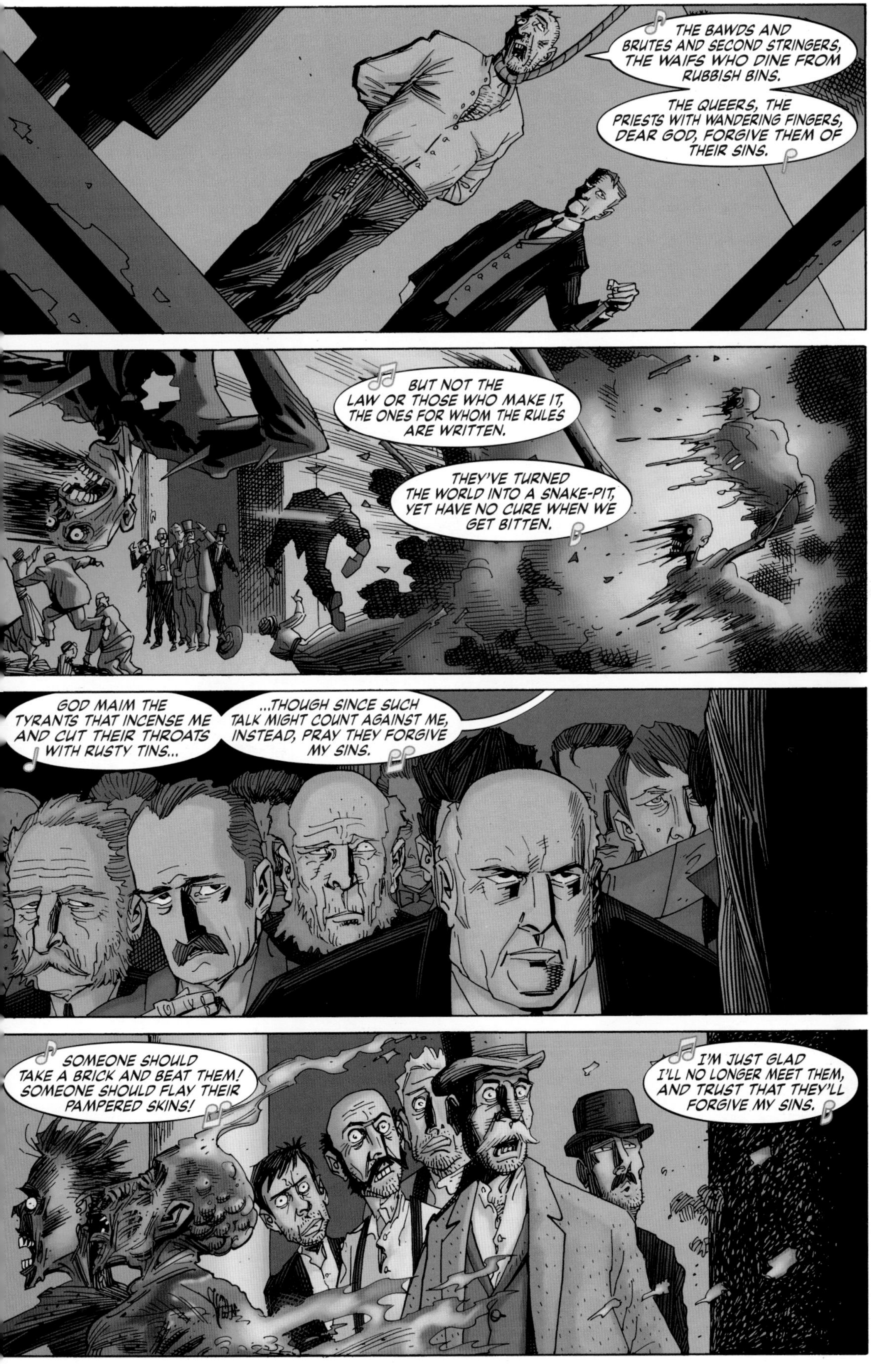
THE BAWDS AND BRUTES AND SECOND STRINGERS, THE WAIFS WHO DINE FROM RUBBISH BINS.
THE QUEERS, THE PRIESTS WITH WANDERING FINGERS, DEAR GOD, FORGIVE THEM OF THEIR SINS.
BUT NOT THE LAW OR THOSE WHO MAKE IT, THE ONES FOR WHOM THE RULES ARE WRITTEN.
THEY'VE TURNED THE WORLD INTO A SNAKE-PIT, YET HAVE NO CURE WHEN WE GET BITTEN.
GOD MAIM THE TYRANTS THAT INCENSE ME AND CUT THEIR THROATS WITH RUSTY TINS...
...THOUGH SINCE SUCH TALK MIGHT COUNT AGAINST ME, INSTEAD, PRAY THEY FORGIVE MY SINS.
SOMEONE SHOULD TAKE A BRICK AND BEAT THEM! SOMEONE SHOULD FLAY THEIR PAMPERED SKINS!
I'M JUST GLAD I'LL NO LONGER MEET THEM, AND TRUST THAT THEY'LL FORGIVE MY SINS.

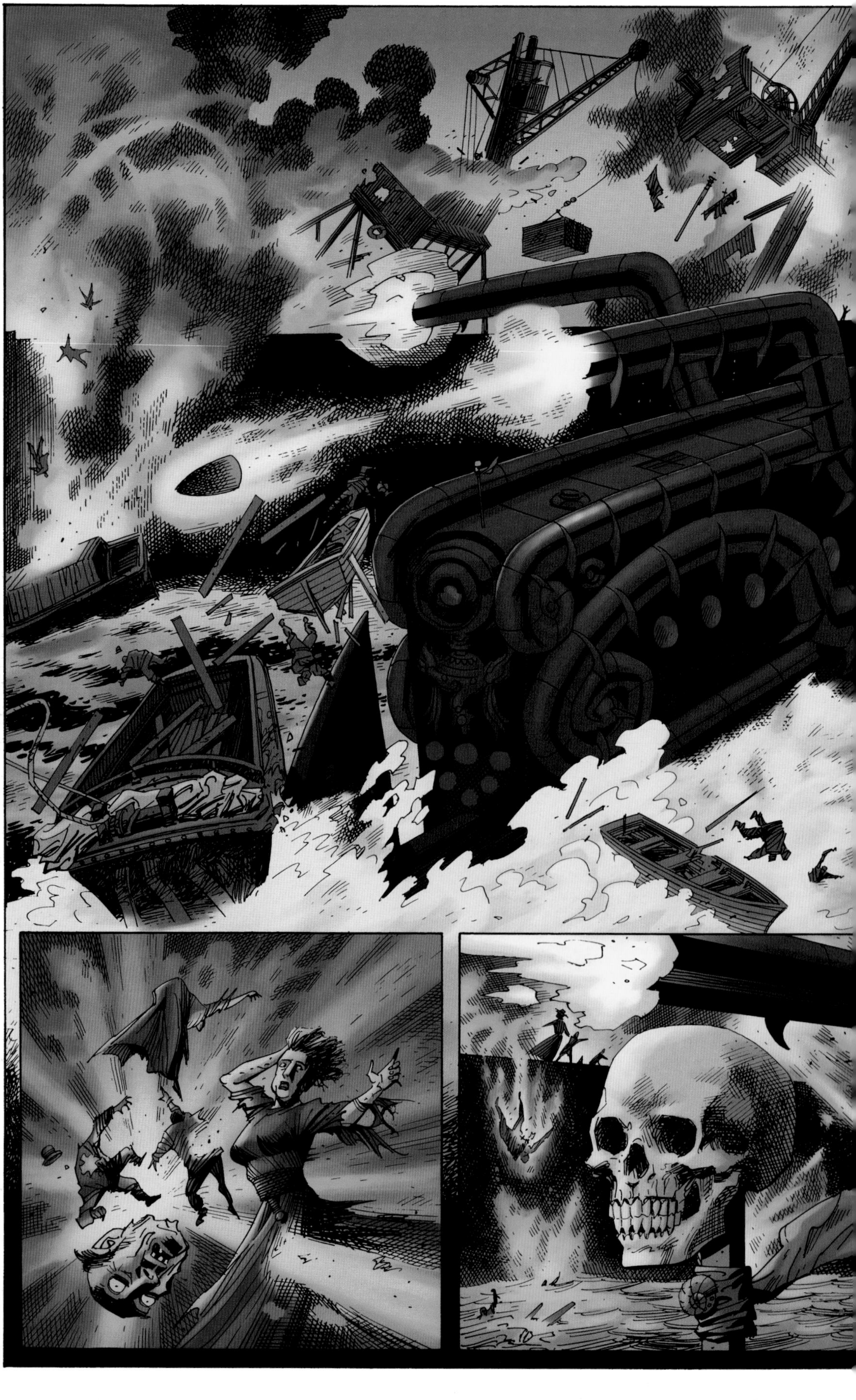

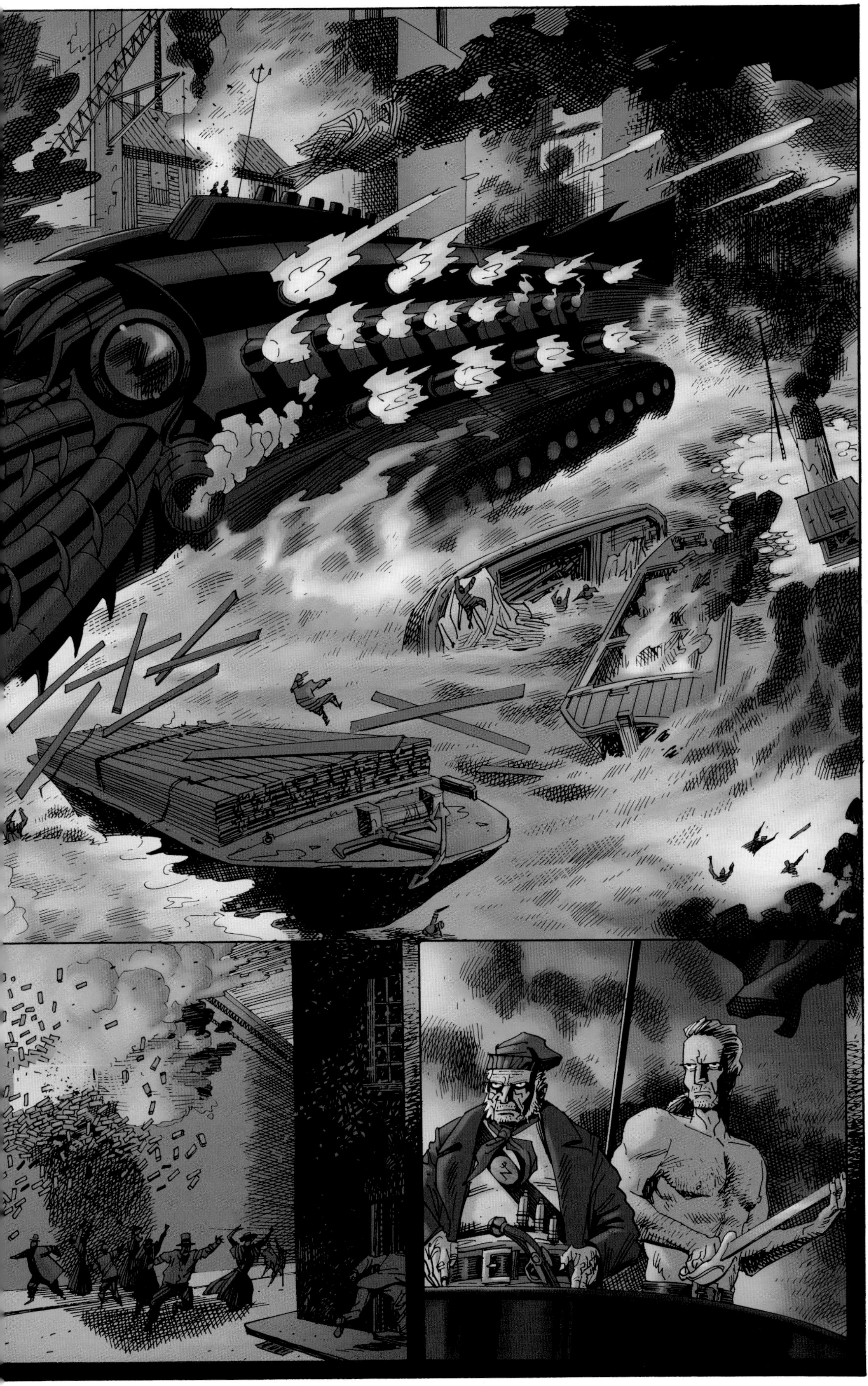

SO, THEN...

IF MR. MACHEATH HAS NO FURTHER LESSONS OR MORAL INSTRUCTIONS FOR US, LET US PROCEED WITH...

M, WAIT! TH-THERE'S A COURIER, SIR. FROM WHITE-HALL...

WHAT?

I-IT'S A MESSAGE CONCERNING THE EARL OF GURNEY, SIR.

Y-YOU BETTER READ IT YOURSELF...

DEAR SUFFERING CHRIST.

MR HOLMES? IS SOMETHING WRONG?

Oh, just a touch.

IT SEEMS THE 14th EARL OF GURNEY HEARD THAT WE'D CAPTURED MacHEATH.

HIS LORDSHIP DIDN'T LIKE THE THOUGHT OF HIS PRIZE KILL BEING TAKEN AWAY FROM HIM, APPARENTLY.

HE'S CONFESSED TO ALL THE WHITECHAPEL MURDERS.

IT'S SIMPLY TOO BAD.

I MEAN, WHAT MORE COULD POSSIBLY GO WRONG?

Um...WELL, ACTUALLY, SIR, THE COURIER SAID SOMETHING ELSE...

WHAT? YOU IMBECILE, WHY DIDN'T YOU TELL ME?

I-IT WASN'T PART OF HIS MESSAGE, SIR.

IT WAS SOMETHING HE HEARD ON HIS WAY HERE...

I-IT'S THE EAST END, SIR.

IT'S UNDER ATTACK BY A WARSHIP.

MY GOD. MY GOD...

O-ORGANIZE THE MILITARY. GET THEM TO THE AREA AT ONCE.

SIR, MY PEOPLE COULD BE THERE MUCH MORE QUICKLY...

YES. GOOD IDEA.

AND YOU PREDICTED A RUTHLESS KILLER ON THE WATERFRONT, DIDN'T YOU?

WHAT A SHAME WE ALL THOUGHT IT WAS MR. MacHEATH.

YOU HEARD HIM, EVERYONE. LET'S FLAG DOWN A COACH AND GET OVER TO THE DOCKS...

wh-WHAT SHOULD WE DO ABOUT MacHEATH, SIR?

YOU MEAN NOW THAT GURNEY'S CONFESSED EVEN TO MURDERS COMMITTED WHILE HE WAS IN THE MADHOUSE?

WE LET HIM GO, I EXPECT.

R-RELEASE MacHEATH, SIR?

WHY NOT?

IT SEEMS THAT IN OUR NEW CENTURY, FORTUNE IS SET TO FAVOUR MR. MacHEATH AND HIS KIND...

...AND MAY HEAVEN HELP US ALL.

♪ Now you think your leg is broke, and you're crawling through the smoke, and a hundred bloody pirates are landing... ♪

♪ ...and their shells have blown the roofs off and demolished every wall, and there's just this one old hotel that they haven't touched at all... ♪

♪ ...so you ask, "Why is that still standing?"

And you ask, "Why is *that* one standing?"

♪ Maybe they've heard, by some sign or some word, there's a grand Lord or Lady living here... ♪

♪ ...and then you see her stepping out into the sunlight, with her hair down, and a rose behind her ear... ♪

♪ ...and the **ship**, the **black raider**, hoists a flag up its masthead and gives a great cheer. ♪

You can't see the sun at all for a choking, smoky pall and the light upon the river is sickly...

...and someone says, "We've had it," and you privately concur because they're rounding up the hostages and dragging them to her, asking her...

KILL THEM SLOW, OR QUICKLY?

Asking *her*, "Kill them slow, or quickly?"

Over the quay it's as quiet as can be, just faint groans and the slop of the tide.

She'll consider a while, then decide...

KILL THEM SLOW.

And as the heads mount, she'll just smile and say...

Huh.

NEXT TIME YOU'LL KNOW ME.

And the ship, the **black raider**, full of plunder and glee...

...prepares for the sea.

GOD, THIS IS HAVOC.

EXCUSE ME, WE'RE AGENTS OF THE CROWN. WHAT ON EARTH'S GOING ON?

LET ME BY! IT'S PIRATES! *HUNDREDS* OF THEM!

PIRATES? WAS HE JOKING? THIS IS THE TWENTIETH CENTURY...

YES, YES, IT IS, ISN'T IT? I KEEP FORGET-TING.

COME ON. LET'S LOOK DOWN...

...here...

I--I DON'T BELIEVE THIS. HALF OF THE DOCKSIDE IS...WELL, IT'S GONE. AND THERE'RE PIRATES *EVERYWHERE*...

GOSH. I LIKE THE SOUND OF THAT.

CHRIST, ORLANDO, DON'T. NOT ON YOUR OWN...

Oh, HUSH. THIS IS THE BLADE OF ENGLAND'S GREATEST DEFENDER.

ONLY UNTIL YOU *STOLE* IT FROM HIM!

MINA, HONESTLY! YOU'RE FOREVER HARPING ON ABOUT THE *PAST.*

LET'S SEE IF I STILL REMEMBER HOW TO DO THIS...

OH, BLOODY HELL! HANG ON, LANDO! WE'RE COMING!

HMM. WELL, ALL RIGHT...

...BUT ONLY IF YOU JOIN THE PIRATES, TO EVEN THINGS UP.

HAHA! *THIS* IS THE LIFE, EH, YOUNG RAFFLES?

BELIEVE ME, I'VE SWASHED A FEW BUCKLES IN MY TIME.

YES. YES, I'LL BET YOU HAVE...

FOR GOD'S SAKE.

FOR GOD'S BLOODY SAKE...

Jack? BROAD-ARROW JACK? A- AND IS THAT THE *NAUTILUS?* WH-WHAT'S HAPPEN-ING?

BLIMEY! MISS...MURRAY, WAS IT?

CAPTAIN, THIS IS...

I KNOW WHO SHE IS.

I SAW HER ONCE BEFORE WHEN SHE FIRST CAME TO OUR ISLAND FOR MY FATHER.

SHE'S THE WOMAN YOU CAUGHT ON THE BEACH.

BUT...THAT WAS TWELVE YEARS AGO, IN 1898. YOU WOULDN'T HAVE BEEN...

MY GOD.

WERE... WERE YOU THAT LITTLE BABY?

WE WERE ALL BABIES ONCE. AND WE ALL GROW UP.

DO YOU KNOW, MY FATHER HAD NOTHING BUT BAD THINGS TO SAY ABOUT YOU?

HIS FOREMOST COMPLAINT WAS THAT YOU WERE A WOMAN. THIS LEADS ME TO SUPPOSE YOU STRONG AND HONOURABLE.

OTHERWISE, I'D HAVE YOU KILLED.

IF YOU TIRE OF ENGLAND AND FANCY THE PIRATE LIFE, SEND WORD.

UNTIL THEN, LEAVE ME ALONE, AND PERHAPS I'LL LEAVE YOU ALONE.

ALL RIGHT, LOOK LIVELY! RECALL THE RAIDING PARTIES AND SEAL THE HATCHES. WE'RE TAKING HER DOWN.

WAIT! I DON'T EVEN KNOW YOUR NAME...

ME?

I'M NO ONE.

PREPARE TO DIVE, MR. MATE.

AYE-AYE, CAPTAIN.

YOU KNOW, ISHMAEL, SHE'S AS BAD AS HER OLD MAN.

HA HA! I'LL TELL YOU WHAT, JACK...

...SHE'S WORSE.

AIN'T IT BLEEDIN' WONDERFUL?

MINA! ARE YOU ALL RIGHT?

W-WE HAD TO TAKE COVER. THEY BROUGHT OUT THESE THINGS LIKE NEMO'S OLD REPEATING HARPOON-PISTOLS...

THAT'S BECAUSE THEY **WERE** NEMO'S PISTOLS.

I THINK I'VE JUST MET HIS SUCCESSOR.

BUGGER ME. I **THOUGHT** THAT LOOKED LIKE THE NAUTILUS. AND YOU MET NEMO'S **SUCCESSOR?** WHAT WAS HE LIKE?

TERRIFYING, ALAN. SHE WAS TERRIFYING.

WE'VE FAILED. WE'VE FAILED TO PREVENT THE DISAS-TER THAT CARNACKI FORESAW...

WITH RESPECT, MINA, WHAT I SAW WAS MUCH WORSE THAN THIS.

I THINK HADDO'S APOCALYPTIC PLAN MAY HAVE YET TO HAPPEN. IT MIGHT BE YEARS. DECADES...

SUPER. AT LEAST WE'VE **THAT** TO LOOK FORWARD TO.

IN THE MEAN-TIME, I'M GOING BACK TO THE MUSEUM.

I'M SICK OF ALL THIS DEATH. I'M **SICK** OF IT.

QUITE FRANKLY, I'M SICK OF US ALL.

LOOKS LIKE THE VISITORS ARE LEAVING, THEN?

Mm. I'M GLAD YOU WEREN'T HUNG FOR YOUR MURDERING, MAC. US GIRLS NEED PROTECTING. THIS WORLD'S TERRIBLE DANGEROUS.

Aye, SUKI. YOU'RE RIGHT.

I SOMETIMES WONDER HOW HUMAN-ITY CONTINUES. **THOSE** DO-GOODERS CERTAINLY AREN'T HELPING MUCH...

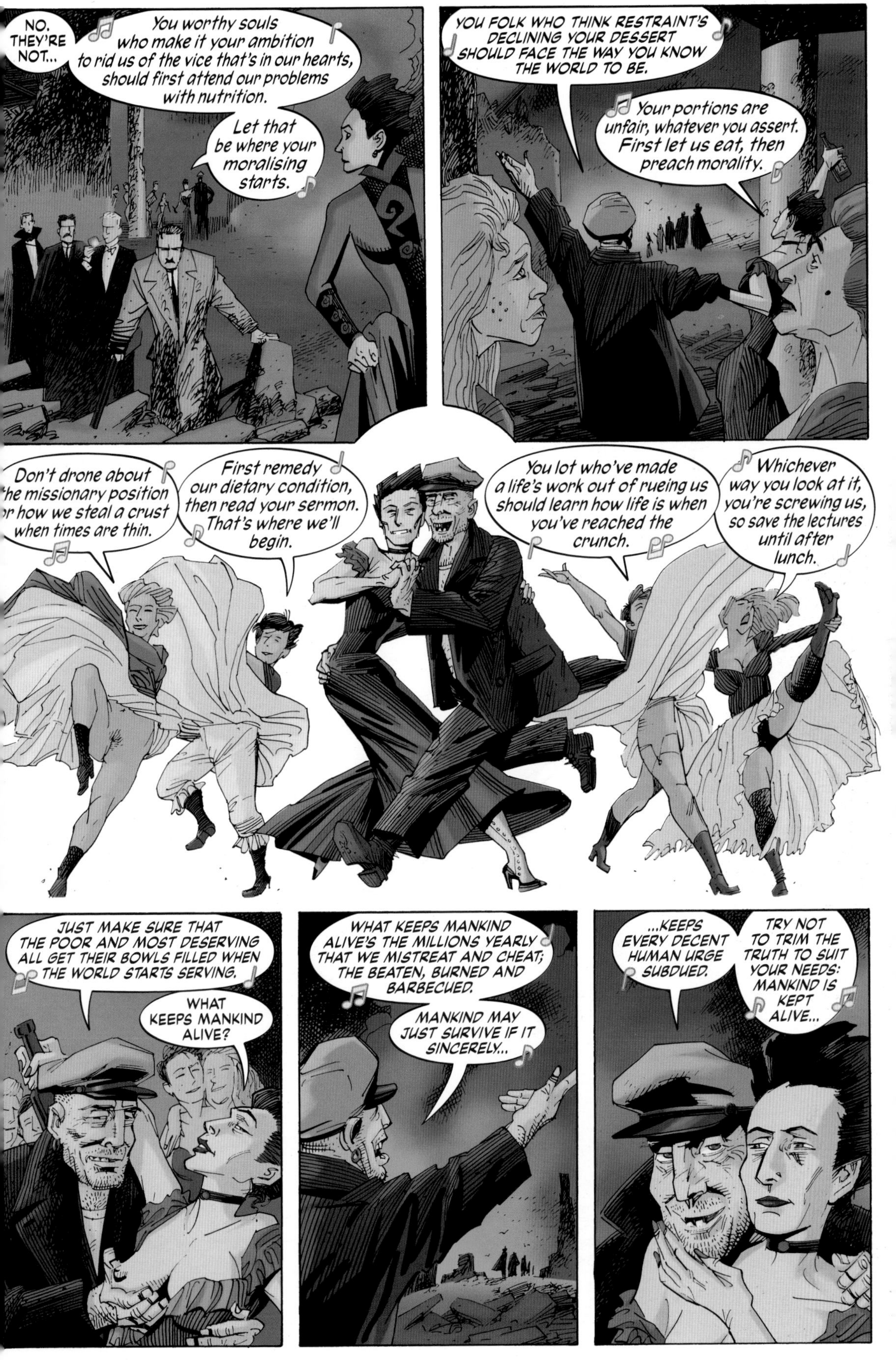
NO. THEY'RE NOT...
You worthy souls who make it your ambition to rid us of the vice that's in our hearts, should first attend our problems with nutrition.
Let that be where your moralising starts.
YOU FOLK WHO THINK RESTRAINT'S DECLINING YOUR DESSERT SHOULD FACE THE WAY YOU KNOW THE WORLD TO BE.
Your portions are unfair, whatever you assert. First let us eat, then preach morality.
Don't drone about the missionary position or how we steal a crust when times are thin.
First remedy our dietary condition, then read your sermon. That's where we'll begin.
You lot who've made a life's work out of rueing us should learn how life is when you've reached the crunch.
Whichever way you look at it, you're screwing us, so save the lectures until after lunch.
JUST MAKE SURE THAT THE POOR AND MOST DESERVING ALL GET THEIR BOWLS FILLED WHEN THE WORLD STARTS SERVING.
WHAT KEEPS MANKIND ALIVE?
WHAT KEEPS MANKIND ALIVE'S THE MILLIONS YEARLY THAT WE MISTREAT AND CHEAT; THE BEATEN, BURNED AND BARBECUED.
MANKIND MAY JUST SURVIVE IF IT SINCERELY...
...KEEPS EVERY DECENT HUMAN URGE SUBDUED.
TRY NOT TO TRIM THE TRUTH TO SUIT YOUR NEEDS: MANKIND IS KEPT ALIVE...

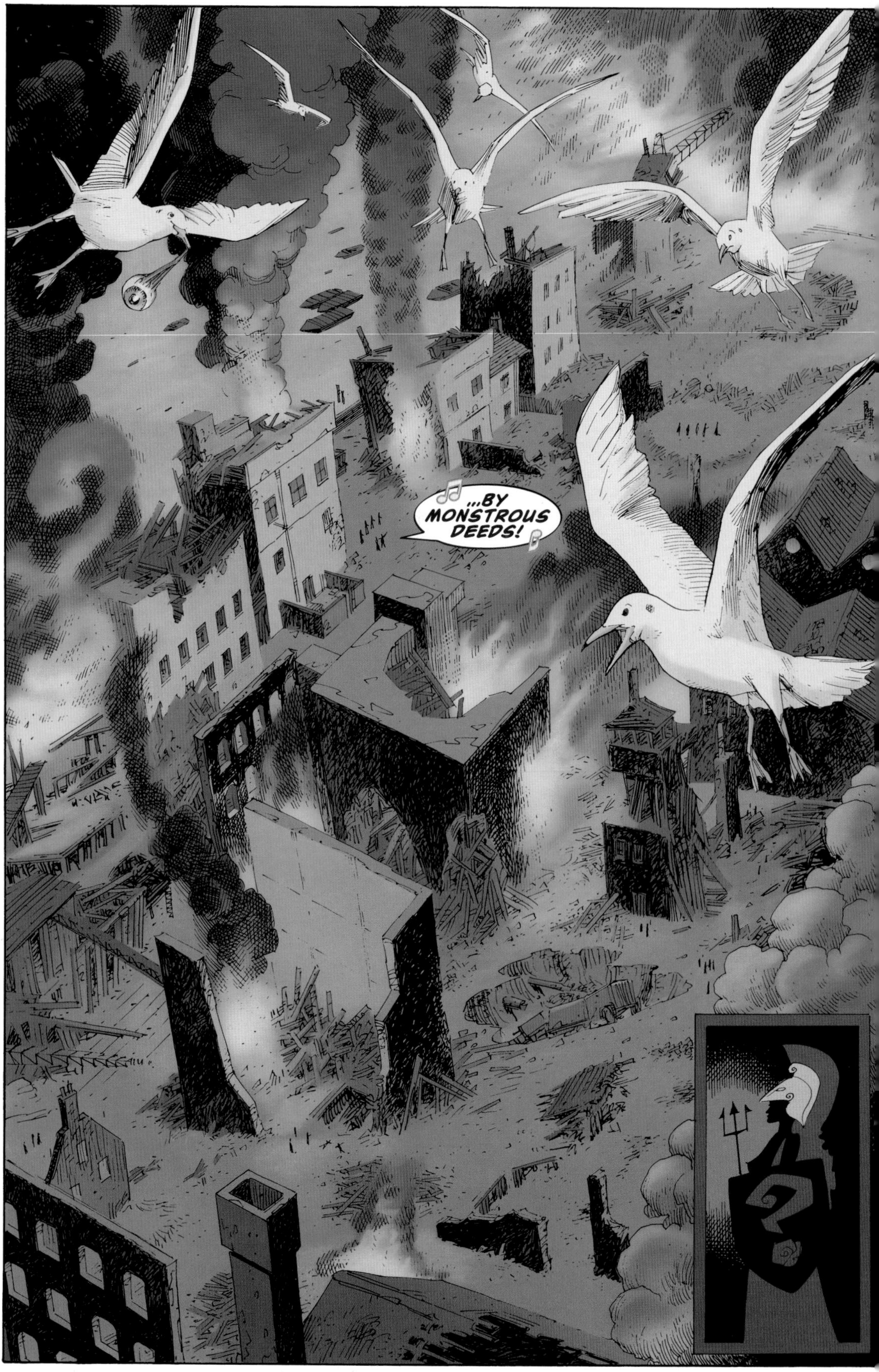
...BY MONSTROUS DEEDS!

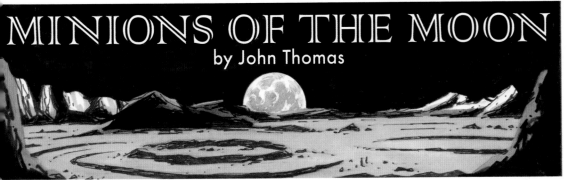

MINIONS OF THE MOON
by John Thomas

(Originally serialised in *Lewd Worlds Science Fiction*, Ed. James Colvin, 183-185, 1969.)

Chapter One: Into The Limbus

The patient shouts and makes a fuss, is held down physically until the sedative they have attempted to re-use begins to take effect. Eventually the furious invective blurs and slobber drips down onto the restraining-jacket's shoulder. Everything breaks into disconnected words, which are dismantled further and reduced to grey, internal fog as consciousness recedes. The patient, by this point, cannot remember where they are, what year it is, or even their precise identity. The eyes slip out of focus, locked upon an icy full moon visible through the ward windows, or it might be the reflection of a light bulb.

Bio of Thebes, Abyssinia, 1236 BC:
Love amongst the Troglodytes

The sand a cooling talcum under her bare feet, she let the hunched and grunting elder lead her out by moonlight from the place where the immortals had their stinking burrows, their secluded town of holes here in the cloaca of humanity.

Bio had live amongst these sullen creatures for some four or five years, ever since she'd seen directions to their settlement carved deep into the rock surround of that strange pool, not far from Punt, filled with a blueness that was neither fire nor water. She had bathed there some nights after her escape from Egypt to East Africa upon an expedition, her abrupt departure brought about by the retraction and eventual inversion of her penis; the enlargement of her breasts. Become a woman she was beautiful, her salty comrades no more to be trusted, though in this she did not blame them. If he'd come across such loveliness a little earlier when she had been a boy, then Bio would have more than likely raped herself. With this in mind she'd fled west and had happened on the luminous lagoon of sapphire plasma, had immersed herself in the cold flames of the undying. On emerging, she had found the stone-etched diagram in the dark by sitting her wet rear upon it as she dried. Weeks later, following the carven map's instructions, she had come to Abyssinia and the pungent settlement of deathless and withdrawn near-animals who had, like she, swum in the azure mere of light, not far from Punt, at various remote points in antiquity. Bored, uncommunicative, these unkempt brutes mostly sat sunk in their pits and their own thoughts while they awaited a death that was clearly never going to arrive.

And yet she stayed there with them, chewed roots and ate grubs with them. She defecated in plain sight as they did and held conversations that were for the most part made of shrugs, sighs, or the raising of a straggly and trailing brow. The truth was that these torpid and subhuman demigods amazed her, filled her to the brim with awe at their solidity, their ancient stillness. They had the charisma not of men and women but of mountains, timeless features of the human landscape that had seen vast glaciers come and go, had heard the crash of fallen stars and stood as witness to uncountable extinctions. In their overpowering scent were untold centuries of cave-dark copulation, mammoth blood and jungle murder. Her current companion, said to be amongst the first of the immortals, was a large and very hairy male who walked upon his furry knuckle-bones almost as often as he did his feet. He sniffed and shuffled, leading her into the Abyssinian night.

He had some days before made her an offer by the means of gesture: he would show to her a great and sacred mystery, if she would let him mount her. This struck her as mythical rather than disagreeable and thus, with her consent, after a further hour of wading through sub-lunar silver they arrived at the appointed place, a desolate expanse of only rocks and fine-milled sand, where both would satisfy their curiosity.

She kneeled in the blonde pumice and he entered her, an act of great ferocity that nearly drove the breath from Bio yet which took but a few seconds to complete, unlike the man-beast's shuddering climax that went on and on until her thighs were trickling with primordial sperm, while both she and her lover howled into the constellations.

When they had rested, he drew her attention to the pieces of black stone about them in the white dust. Upon close inspection these were made from something she had not before encountered, a unique material that seemed to drink light, giving back no glitter or reflection. Some shards, furthermore, had smoothly crafted corners. Pinned beneath the detumescent primitive, she reached out with one hand to touch a midnight splinter.

Thoughts and images thrummed through her like a lightning-shock. Pre-human savages at time's dawn gaping in religious terror at the great square-cut black stone that stands there in their midst, the bravest creeping hesitantly forth to place a hand upon it. A cascade of information, fire and numbers, wheels and tools and weapons. Years later, its unfathomable work completed, the black block spontaneously shatters and is all but lost beneath the drifts of aeons…

She let the jet fragment tumble from her hand. Behind her, still inside her, the immortal cupped her face and lifted it. As though imparting a great secret, first he pointed to the sharp obsidian chips surrounding their joined bodies. Then he pointed to the moon.

**Mina and Allan, Bloomsbury, 1910:
In the Wake of the Black Nautilus**

He found her in their quarters at the museum, in its locked wing. She'd been crying, a release for all the dockside horrors of the afternoon, and when he sat down quietly beside her on their bed at first she shouted at him angrily, then cried some more.

'You didn't talk to her or see her eyes. They were so cold, and she was no more than fifteen years old. What can have happened to her that had killed her girlhood and replaced it with the mantle of her father? It wasn't the heads and slaughter that upset me half so much as that poor child, become a monster before she's become a woman.'

When he placed his arm protectively around her shoulders she at least did not flinch back from him, and they sat there in silence for some moments. He reflected that they were alone in the museum, in that vast space full of silent, ancient things. Orlando, after all the bloodshed on the wharf, had been much too excited to return to their headquarters and was very likely out carousing in the dives of the East End. Carnacki and the burglar Raffles, both in darker and more sober moods, had each retired home to their separate addresses and their highly individual lives. It was just him and Mina again now.

'Darling, I'm sorry for the mess we made of things with Haddo, and for all the stupid things that Lando said. We acted like a gang of idiots and everything went straight to hell as a result.'

She tilted back her head, and her jade eyes gazed up at him.

'It wasn't your fault. It would all have gone to hell as quickly if we'd done things my way. I was being unfair, blaming you. I think the truth of it is that I'm starting to feel overwhelmed by the enormity of knowing that we're going to live forever, like Orlando, ever since we took our dip in that Ugandan pool. It all seemed like a marvellous lark at first, like something from a fairy story, but just recently the thought of it has come to haunt me. I feel so small, Allan. I feel like I'm standing all alone upon the threshold of eternity. And if it's like this now, what will it be like in a hundred or a thousand years?"

He pulled her to him, stroking her black hair to soothe her, and to soothe himself. He knew exactly what she meant, had felt the same sense of unease since stepping from the blue fires of that strange African pool and finding himself young again, a strapping fellow in his early twenties with a lifetime's scars erased... or at least most of them. He'd found he still bore the faint signs of injuries sustained in boyhood, and of course the awful marks on Mina's throat had not been wiped away. Perhaps the blue fires had restored them to their prime, with any damages they had incurred prior to that point remaining unaffected? Allan didn't know. He only knew that he shared his beloved's apprehensions of their new immortal state, but had not managed to define those fears as clearly or succinctly as had she. He murmured to her and, again, it was as much to reassure himself as comfort her. About them was the dark of the museum, millennia deep.

'I've had the same thoughts, darling, but I promise you, you're not alone. If you're standing upon the threshold of eternity, then I'll be standing there beside you. Mina, you are everything to me. I love you and I promise you I always will.'

Her eyes still brimming, Mina favoured him with a sad smile.

'Always is a bigger word now than it was five years ago, my handsome hero. You may as well promise me the moon.'

He laughed, and gestured out through the tall windows of their bedroom at the bloated silver orb that hung like a Montgolfier balloon in the black heavens south of Oxford Street.

'What, that one? The one shining on the rotting cabbage leaves that choke the gutters along Berwick Street. The one that lights the drunk newspaper-writer's way from the Pillars of Hercules down to the Coach and Horses? Well, if that's the one you want, my love, then you shall have it. Upon my apparently eternal life, I hereby promise you the moon that's over Soho.'

Despite herself Mina was laughing with him now, her vision of the chilly, endless halls of Time beginning to recede, her dread abating. After all, perhaps Allan was right. Perhaps their love would be enough to outlast empires, outlast worlds. It seemed like long odds but it was at least a ray of hope that she could cling to, bright although remote and distant, like the gibbous satellite above the boozy brothels of that ancient neighborhood.

**Allan and Orlando, Paris, 1964:
Her Long, Adorable Lashes**

She lowered her subtly-painted eyes submissively while her demanding lover placed his hand upon her stockinged knee, there in the rear seat of a chauffer-driven limousine as it nosed through the outskirts of the intricately-textured city. It was a new game that they were playing, an experiment intended to enliven their extremely long relationship. Part of the game was that she should not call him by his name, and only speak when she was spoken to. In turn, he would refer to her only by her initial.

They were trying to continue the erotic European odysseys that they had read of in the journals of their 18th-century predecessors, and were travelling at present to a terribly exclusive gentlemen's establishment somewhere amongst the labrynthine streets. Once hey'd arrived, her lover would deliver her into a thrill-ingly demeaning form of sexual slavery, to be used and abused by the perverse members as they liked. Know-ing them for descendants of the decadent aristocrats of Silling whom she'd heard her long-dead colleague Percy Blakeny speak of once, she shivered with a mixture of desire and dread to think of being owned by them, in that most intimate of manners. Sitting there beside her on the creaking leather rear seat of the car, so cold against her thighs, her lover turned and spoke, moving his hand along her sheer hose as he did so.

'It's a shame our mutual ladyfriend decided that she didn't want to travel with us, isn't it? It's almost as though she were making out that she's above this sort of thing, when we both know she isn't. Or at least, she's not when she's in the right mood, though it's been ages since that last occurred. I don't think that it's happened since that marvellous long night you showed us in the Blazing World, when we were just back from the wretched business that surrounded the Black Dossier, and that was, what, six years ago?'

His hand had by now reached beneath her dress's hem and was exploring at the lace-ensconced and sultry delta. She said nothing, but sat trembling with delight as he continued with his deceptively casual conversation. In the rear-view mirror she could see their silent driver's darting eyes as he watched while her lover fondled her.

'Of course, she's off having her own adventures with a lot of men and women in peculiar costumes, so I don't expect that ours would interest her. Quite frankly, I don't think her new secret society…"The Seven Stars," wasn't it called?…sounds half as interesting as the fraternity we're on our way to meet. Speaking of which, I've got a sudden urge to see your bottom, while it still officially belongs to me. Take off your underthings and give them to me, as a souvenir.'

Heart hammering, enflamed as much by her own harem-girl obedience as by the good-looking young man's deliberately gruff, commanding tone, she did as she was told. The chauffer's furtive eyes glinted salaciously in the mirror as she lifted up her backside from the sticky seat and took down the requested items. Glimpsing her white rear, perfectly round as framed by the black stocking tops, her lover made the obvious lunar comparison. The car drove on and O. sat with her lovely eyelids lowered, staring at the automobile's carpeted interior, not daring to look up at him unless he asked her to.

Vull and Captain Universe, Stardust's Tomb, the Lesser Magellanic Cloud, 1964: Requiem for a Space-Wizard

The two super-adventurers, of whom but one was visible, stood framed by the stupendous airlock threshold of the hollow sun. The Captain, in his rose-and-primrose uniform, turned to the empty air beside him with a smile. Thanks to his absolute awareness of the cosmos, granted by the science-god Galileo, he could just make out the otherwise unseen form of his colleague standing next to him, the long cloak and the weird, shadowy helmet of Vull the Invisible picked out in flickering phosphorescent lines. From this translu-cent, shimmering mirage it was impossible to draw any conclusions as to Vull's identity, other than the impression of a slight and slender man whose age was indeterminate. Universe knew his friend to have been

thwarting evil-doers in the early 1930s, long before the Captain's own career had had its origin, and thus supposed that his companion must be in his fifties or his sixties. He clapped one hand on Vull's scrawny, cape-draped shoulder and asked the blank space for its opinion of the stunning infra-stellar headquarters that Captain Universe had taken from another costumed superman in planet-pulverising mortal combat.

'Well? What do you think? You must admit, it's a bit roomier than your Star Chamber down beneath Fitzrovia. The being who constructed it was a demented megalomaniac, of course, but since I redesigned the place I rather like it.'

Vull stood silent for a moment and then made reply, the deep and echoing tones issuing from nowhere with an almost electronic resonance around the edges of the sound. Universe wondered, and not for the first time, if his fellow hero might not be other than human, perhaps a sophisticated robot or a visitor come from some distant world.

'It's unbelievable. What are these funny rounded screens on stalks that seem to sprout from every sur-face? Are they your additions, or did they come with the property?'

The Captain, listening carefully to Vull's speech pat-terns, revised his opinion. The idiosyncrasies betrayed the speaker as an ordinary human rather than an android or a spaceman, but suggested that the senior member of The Seven Stars might be effeminate, which was to Universe's way of seeing things a more alarming possibility. Attempting to dispel this thoroughly unwel-come and surely uncharitable notion, he steered his invisible companion deeper into the astounding depths of the star-fortress as he answered.

'No, those are the former occupant's invention. They're a range of monitors or scanners that enabled him to view any location in the galaxy, including places in dimensions other than our own. One of them even looks into an utterly unheard-of astronomical phenom-enon, a kind of hole or pocket in the fabric of space-time itself, inhabited by a grotesque thing that he called a "Headless Head-hunter." The blighter tried to throw me into it during our battle, but he wasn't quite as powerful as he thought he was. I left the view-screens where they were when I remodelled the remainder of this artificial star's interior. You never know when they might come in handy. Anyway, let me guide you around. I can show you the man himself, if you've a mind to see him.'

Again, the low, somehow electronic tones emerged from nothingness.

'I thought you said that he was dead. I thought you said you'd killed him.'

Leading his unseen guest over gleaming marble floors between spectacular and self-invented towers of inscrutable equipment or past huge and cryptic trophies from his own fantastic exploits, Universe gave an am-biguous shrug of his broad shoulders.

'It depends on what you mean by dead. You have to understand that this so-called Space Wizard was a brutal and sadistic monster. He preferred to punish adversaries with a fiendishly inventive range of living deaths, so that they could suffer eternally. I gave the power-crazed thug a taste of his own medicine, that's all.'

He gestured to the wall-sized portal made from foot-thick glass that their perambulations had been

Once more there was a pause before the strange metallic voice made its enquiry.

'What were you fighting over? Were you working under the instruction of your employers at the United Nations?'

Captain Universe looked grim and shook his auburn head.

'The U.N. aren't the only force I answer to. My powers were given to me by a quintet of science-mystics who've transcended space and time, Pythagoras and Leonardo being counted in that number. These beings exist, along with other awesome presences, upon a level of reality beyond the confines of the mortal realm. Archimedes, Aristotle, and even more recent sub-atomic physicists such as the Swedish theoretician Borghelm. Our friend in the ice-block was attempting to force his way into that sublime elite, and I was given the command to stop him. It's that simple.'

Turning from the eerie exhibit, the pair walked back across the fake sun's cavernous interior, their conversation moving onto other matters.

'Vull, I'm sorry about how The Seven Stars worked out after our one and only victory against the 'Mass. I told my brother Jet about it and he was appalled. That thing might once have been one of his colleagues. Everyone feels bad about what happened.'

Vull, responding, sounded disappointed and yet philosophical.

'I know. I had high hopes for all of us, but now Mars Man and Satin have been forced to drop from sight along with all our other difficulties, I don't think it's possible to put things right. Besides, like you, I'm answerable to higher powers and currently have other matters to attend to. Could I ask you to return me to our home-world in your spaceship? More specifically, I need to rendezvous with representatives of the supernal forces that I mentioned at a ruined castle in the north of Scotland.'

Universe smiled and said he thought that it might be arranged.

It was, astonishingly, less than three days later that Vull stood upon the grassy slopes of crumbling Dunbayne Castle, watching for the halo-flash of rippling radiance high in the blue dome of the upper atmosphere that would mean Captain Universe's craft had broken the light-barrier and was on its way home towards the distant nebulae. When this had taken place, Vull sat upon the turf and waited for perhaps an hour or more before a wholly different means of transportation drifted into view above the northerly horizon. Even from this distance, the invisible adventurer could see the rising pink flecks that were a by-product of the pataphysically-constructed vessel's flower-powered engine.

Taking off the helmet of invisibility and startling some nearby sheep by suddenly appearing in their midst, Vull shook her long black hair down to her shoulders and awaited the arrival of the Rose of Nowhere.

leading to. There on the massive window's further side was what appeared to be a chamber filled with an unusually clear and transparent type of ice. Suspended as if floating at its centre was the freakish form of the defeated superman, an almost human entity some eight feet long from head to crown, clad in a skin-tight suit of lurid turquoise. It had far too many ribs and an abnormal musculature, with parts that were wildly disparate in their proportions. The exaggeratedly long head was topped with blonde hair that had frozen into spikes of an unnaturally bright yellow. While Vull stared in silence at the icebound giant, Captain Universe explained as best he could.

'The substance he's encased in is a frozen form of poly-water that he called Ice-9, and he had one or two unfortunates entombed within it when I tracked him back here to this lair for his last stand. I'll swear that he was drunk for that concluding showdown. You could smell the liquor on his breath and he was stumbling and uncoordinated, otherwise I doubt I could have thrown him into his own icy chamber of eternal torment quite as easily as was in fact the case.'

Prospero and his operatives, the Blazing World, 1964: Coming Forth by Day

Over the ornamental root-garden there shone the thousand suns that give this realm its name. The tall and bearded figure in exquisite robes, born to Italian aristocracy some centuries before, peered through the jade and garnet lenses of his pince-nez at the company assembled on the ageless terraces before him. Four in number, they sat perched upon wide benches carved from single pieces of obsidian that had the staring eye motif which was the emblem of the Blazing World inlaid as a mosaic of alabaster. In the star-crammed sky above, an Owl-man in a cut silk tunic screeched and whooped exuberantly.

Seated by herself on the bench closest to the magus was the marvellously wilful lady music-teacher, Wilhelmina Murray, who had so impressively commanded the third incarnation of that league he'd founded all those years ago. Clad in a single figure-hugging garment of jet black with cape and leather boots and gloves to match, she sat with an unusual bulb-topped helmet resting in her lap, gazing attentively at Prospero through goggles that had eyes of different colours, blankly staring discs of red and green.

The three remaining members of the band that the former Duke of Milan had lately summoned sat together on a separate couch of polished stone. These were two living wooden dolls named Peg and Sara Jane, along with the unnaturally squat and massive figure who was both their lover and commander. If this star-ling and yet engaging creature had a given name it was not known to the magician. Brought here to this dazzling fourth-dimensional domain by Queen Olympia of nearby Toyland, the wild-maned black aeronaut had introduced himself to Prospero as 'a cummun Galley-wag.' From this the wizard had surmised his guest to be perhaps an escaped slave, come from a hidden cosmos that was by some means concealed from ordinary scrutiny. That this supposed world and its occupants were formed from matter of far greater density than that which made the earthly plane was evidenced by the fine cracks appearing in the solid block of carved obsidian upon which the extra-terrestrial freebooter sat, his thick legs kicking idly, far too short to reach the ground. Being essentially organic in his nature despite the discrepancies of his material composition, the dark-matter buccaneer wore spectacles with mismatched lenses, like Miss Murray. His two literal playthings, on the other hand, were ani-manikins constructed on the principles established by the late Dr. Copelius and thus did not require the same corrective eyewear. Both clad in short summer dresses that appeared to have been fashioned from the flag of the United States, the two impossibly slim wooden figurines sat giggling and talking kittenishly to each other with trilling falsettos in a language which the magus recognised as Dutch. The conjuror's assembled crew were clearly growing restless as they waited for him to explain the reason for his urgent summoning. He cleared his throat, and then began.

'No doubt thou wouldst hear why I called thee hence: what grave calamity requires thine aid. Know then that this be not an earthly woe, but, rather, it afflicts another sphere.'

Prospero gestured with one ring-decked hand, heavy with chryosprase and tourmaline, and in the air before them there appeared a vision of an unmistakable pale orb against a field of sequinned night. The Galley-wag tilted his huge head quizzically.

'By the great quim o' singularity! Be that not your whirl's loon-lamp?'

The elderly mage and young music teacher felt as much as heard the creature's voice, with its inhumanly low register reverberating in their bellies and the marrow of their bones. Prospero nodded and, with one extended fingertip, touched the diaphanous and shimmering image in some half-a-dozen places, leaving a red dot of pulsing phosphorescence at each point of contact.

'Aye, ebon navigator of the void, it is the moon I conjure to plain sight. There, marked in crimson, see Earth's colonies, where fly the stiff and windless flags of France, of England, Germany, America. Yet are there conflicts in those cratered lands that are not born of earthly enmities. Two species native to that silv'ry ball have lately clashed together in a war which, ranging far across the lunar globe, endangers the terrestrial settlements. I fear that if these battles should persist, Earth's settlers shall be forced to relocate unto a certain area of that sphere where we wouldst rather that they ventured not, not until it is the appointed time there at the dawn of a new century. I charge thee to set sail, then, for night's jewel, there to placate these warring lunar tribes that our Blazing World's schemes go not awry.'

Miss Murray raised one black-gloved hand, and Prospero permitted her to speak.

'Most noble Duke, might I ask why my colleagues Allan and Orlando were not summoned to this meeting? Are they not to journey with us?'

The enchanter shook his head. Across the terraces, a sun that had a wry and sleepy smile was setting over diamond quays and ululating minarets.

'They undertake an amorous idyll in Europe's dens of pain and ecstasy, unwilling or unable to respond to all my imprecations and demands. I fear I know my former squire of old, lascivious and truant in her way, and hazard we shall see no more of her nor of thy youthful huntsman paramour until their lusty chase hath run its course.'

The music teacher, rising from her bench, pursed her lips disapprovingly.

'I see. Then we may as well board the Rose of Nowhere and make ready to embark as soon as possible. I bid you a good aeon, Prince of Necromancers.'

Prospero watched as the odd quartet walked off across the ornamental gardens, with the Galley-wag leaving behind him webs of crack and fracture on the paving stones in lieu of footprints. The twin doll-girls held hands as they skipped together with their flag-skirts flaring, chattering excitedly in Dutch, and only Wilhelmina Murray seemed disheartened. With her long cloak trailing mournfully and the outlandish helmet underneath her arm she strode away between fantastic topiaries. The magician gestured, and the evocation of the moon floating beside him fell apart into a billion scintillating motes. Chewing the ends of his moustache, he hoped that this was not an omen.

Mina and the Galley-wag, the Rose of Nowhere, 1964: Huckleberry Friends

Wearing the borrowed costume of a long-deceased Vull the Invisible she stood there on the deck, gripping the rail and marvelling that she could still respire although their boat had sailed beyond the thinnest reaches of Earth's upper atmosphere some half an hour before. Admittedly the air she breathed was scented heavily with roses, a by-product of the craft's unusual method of propulsion, but this was scarcely a hardship.

Behind them, her home planet was a stupefying opal while ahead was an infinity of ink where countless flakes of furnace-light hung in suspension. Somewhere down below, in the beguiling swirl and mottle of the blue world's cloud and ocean, she knew that her friends pursued their earthly lives as usual. Fathoms beneath the great sprawl of the sea, an ageing savage beauty known as Jenny Nemo would be lighting candles at the starboard shrine of her night-black submersible in memory of her late husband, the dependable Broad-Arrow Jack. Elsewhere within the seabed-grazing vessel, Jenny's daughter Hira would still be asleep in the next cabin to her own child, Jenny's grandson. Not yet six, Jack Dakkar was the fruit of an arranged dynastic union between his mother and the since-deceased air-pirate Armand Robur, a descendant of the more notorious Jean. Much as she'd liked the little boy when they had met, Mina could not help thinking that he represented a potentially explosive mix of lethal bloodstocks.

Then, of course, there were her other comrades. There was witty and ingenious Queen Olympia with her brooding consort in the snow-surrounded pocket of eternal summer known as Toyland. At their various secret bases or their alias day-jobs there were Captain Universe and the few other super-people who where left from Mina's recent incognito and foredoomed attempt to form a band of champions, while somewhere in the demimonde of Paris were her lovers, Allan and the pulchritudinous Orlando, hurling themselves into a debauch in an attempt to dull the dread that came with immortality.

Her reverie was interrupted by a doleful and protesting creak from the ship's black-material timbers,

somewhere close behind her. Turning, Mina found herself confronted by the Galley-wag. Like her, he had dispensed with the two-coloured spectacles now that they were no longer in the 4-D territories of the Blazing World, and the white saucers of his lidless eyes shone from the unreflective dark globe of his shaggy head as he addressed her formally, according to his own conventions.

'Bread and tits, resplendent swan of Peril! Does yer bezoms heave fer home?'

The subterranean pitch of his inhuman voice made the dark metal of the handrail hum in resonance. Mina smiled fondly as she ventured a reply in the same idiom.

'Bread and tits to *you*, brave rider on the night's starry pudendum. No, I wasn't homesick. I was thinking about all the people that we're leaving back on Earth, behind us. I suppose that I was feeling a bit…oh! I say, what's that, just off the port bow?'

The ethereal mariner swivelled his massive cranium to peer in the direction she had indicated. Mina noticed, quite irrelevantly, that he had a bottle tucked into the red sash of his belt. She fleetingly supposed this to be rum of an unworldly distillation. Something glittering approached them, tumbling through trans-planetary gloom and coruscating as it came, as though lit by its own internal fire.

'Why, by my tripes! It books to be a lantern-cadaver encubed in frusticles!'

As the trajectory of the revolving and illuminated mass began to take it under the ascending Rose of Nowhere, Mina gasped. It was a lump of ice, and at its heart was a contorted, black-clad corpse still clinging to a ball of greenish radiance. As the refrigerated mass rotated she found herself gazing into the eternally-unblinking, horror-stricken eyes of her late adversary, the depraved professor of mathematics, spymaster and criminal, James Moriarty. His gaunt features, locked in a last breathless scream, were under-lit by the crepuscular glow of the Cavorite clutched to his frozen breast. Then the corpse-satellite was gone, fallen away beneath their vessel to continue its unending orbit.

Hesitantly, still stunned by this unexpected meeting with her former foe, Mina communicated what she knew of the dead, icebound figure to her host. The Galley-wag gave a low, sympathetic growl that fractured a glass dial in his array of instruments.

'He sounds to be a noxic vile-guard, an' yer whirl's well rid o' hum. Now, wishin' no intrudence, I'd stamped herewards to bequire if you were wantin' blanket-company amid this wendless vastard of a night? I know as Sarey-Jane's taken a varnish to yer since you lost yer blondery, if you were in a mood fer sallymappin'. Alsewise, yer'd be wellcum bunked betwixt me an' the twin of 'um.'

Realising that she'd been politely propositioned and belatedly identifying the glass bottle jutting from the Galley-wag's red sash as being filled with linseed oil rather than an exotic rum, Mina felt both obscurely flattered and amused as she respectfully declined his invitation. Taking no offence, the baryonic buccaneer returned below decks to his greased and squeaking love-toys, leaving Mina with her thoughts and the indifferent canopy of stars. Ahead of them, beyond the Rose of Nowhere's shark-faced prow, a golf-ball moon inflated steadily across the next few hours until it filled the firmament from rim to rim.

– To Be Continued –